Praise for *Mon*

"In this unforgettable, surprisingly hilarious memoir, journalist and professor Smith chronicles his head-clanging, flop-sweating battles with acute anxiety. . . . He's clear-eyed and funny about his condition's painful absurdities."

—*People* (four stars)

"This book will change the way you think about anxiety. . . . Daniel Smith's writing dazzled me. . . . Painful experiences are described with humor, and complex ideas are made accessible. . . . *Monkey Mind* is a rare gem."

—*Pittsburgh Post-Gazette*

"*Monkey Mind* [is] fleet, funny, and productively exhausting."

—Ben Greenman, *The New York Times Book Review*

"You'll laugh out loud many times during Daniel Smith's *Monkey Mind*. . . . In the time-honored tradition of leavening pathos with humor, Smith has managed to create a memoir that doesn't entirely let him off the hook for bad behavior . . . but promotes understanding of the similarly afflicted."

—*O Magazine*

"Smith does a skillful job of dissecting the mechanics of anxiety as well as placing the reader in his fitful shoes."

—*Publishers Weekly*

"*Monkey Mind* [is] a balance of the devastating and the devastatingly hilarious. As Smith traces his ongoing battle with clinical anxiety, we learn just how disruptive and downright crippling the struggle can be—and how difficult it can be to acknowledge and diagnose, let alone begin to understand and treat."

—ScientificAmerican.com

"[Smith] adroitly dissects his relentless mental and physical symptoms with intelligence and humor. . . . [An] intimate and touching journey through one man's angst-ridden life."

—*The Star Tribune* (Minneapolis)

"Here's one less thing for Daniel Smith to worry about: He sure can write. In *Monkey Mind,* a memoir of his lifelong struggles with anxiety, he defangs the experience with a winning combination of humor and understanding."

—Heller McAlpin, NPR.org

"For fellow anxiety-sufferers, it's like finding an Anne of Green Gables–style kindred spirit."

—*New York* magazine's Vulture.com

"[*Monkey Mind*] will be recognized in the years to come as the pre-eminent first-person narrative of the anxiously lived life."

—*Psychiatric Times*

"The book is one man's story, but at its core it's about all of us."

—*Booklist*

"A true treasure-trove of insight laced with humor and polished prose."

—*Kirkus Reviews* (starred)

"I read *Monkey Mind* with admiration for its bravery and clarity. Daniel Smith's anxiety is matched by a wonderful sense of the comic, and it is this which makes *Monkey Mind* not only a dark, pain-filled book but a hilariously funny one, too. I broke out into explosive laughter again and again."

—Oliver Sacks, bestselling author of
The Mind's Eye and *Musicophilia*

"You don't need a Jewish mother, or a profound sweating problem, to feel Daniel Smith's pain in *Monkey Mind*. His memoir treats what must be the essential ailment of our time—chronic anxiety—and it does so with wisdom, honesty, and the kind of belly laughs that can only come from troubles transformed."

—Chad Harbach, author of *The Art of Fielding*

"Daniel Smith maps the jagged contours of anxiety with such insight, humor, and compassion that the result is, oddly, calming. There are countless gems in these pages, including a fresh take on the psychopathology of chronic nail biting, an ill-fated ménage á trois—and the funniest perspiration scene since Albert Brooks's sweaty performance in *Broadcast News*. Read this book. You have nothing to lose but your heart palpitations, and your Xanax habit."

—Eric Weiner, author of *The Geography of Bliss*

"I don't know Daniel Smith, but I do want to give him a hug. His book is so bracingly honest, so hilarious, so sharp, it's clear there's one thing he doesn't have to be anxious about: whether or not he's a great writer."

—A.J. Jacobs, author of *Drop Dead Healthy*
and *The Year of Living Biblically*

"Daniel Smith has written a wise, funny book, a great mix of startling memoir and fascinating medical and literary history, all of it delivered with humor and a true generosity of spirit. I only got anxious in the last part, when I worried the book would end. Of course, it did, but Smith's hopeful last chapters helped me cope."

—Sam Lipsyte, author of *Home Land* and *The Ask*

ALSO BY DANIEL SMITH

Muses, Madmen, and Prophets: Hearing Voices and the Borders of Sanity

monkey mind

a memoir of anxiety

daniel smith

Simon & Schuster Paperbacks

New York London Toronto Sydney New Delhi

Simon & Schuster Paperbacks
A Division of Simon & Schuster, Inc.
1230 Avenue of the Americas
New York, NY 10020

First Simon & Schuster trade paperback edition June 2013

SIMON & SCHUSTER PAPERBACKS and colophon are registered trademarks of Simon & Schuster, Inc.

For information about special discounts for bulk purchases, please contact Simon & Schuster Special Sales at 1-866-506-1949 or business@simonandschuster.com.

The Simon & Schuster Speakers Bureau can bring authors to your live event. For more information or to book an event, contact the Simon & Schuster Speakers Bureau at 1-866-248-3049 or visit our website at www.simonspeakers.com.

Designed by Akasha Archer

Manufactured in the United States of America

20   19   18   17   16   15   14   13   12

The Library of Congress has cataloged the hardcover edition as follows:
Smith, Daniel, date.
   Monkey mind : a memoir of anxiety / Daniel Smith.
      p.   cm.
   1. Smith, Daniel, date—Mental health.   2. Anxiety disorders.   3. Mentally ill—United States—Biography.   I. Title.
   RC464.S59A3 2012
   616.85'220092—dc23
   [B]   2011025971
ISBN 978-1-4391-7730-3
ISBN 978-1-4391-7731-0 (pbk)
ISBN 978-1-4391-7732-7 (ebook)

Author's note: The events described in this book are as real as I could manage. Certain names and details have been changed to protect me from legal and emotional ramifications, which, trust me, aren't fun. Also: memory is unstable. We do our best.

Grateful acknowledgment is made for art on the following pages. Page 119: "Here I and Sorrow Sit," drawing by William James, Houghton Library, Harvard University, call number MS Am 1092.2 (55). Page 120: Lion tamer, chromolithograph, Gibson & Co. (Cincinnati, Ohio), published c. 1873.

I don't know what is the matter with him, and the doctors don't know what is the matter with him, and he doesn't know himself what is the matter with him. We all say it's on the nerves, and we none of us know what we mean when we say it.
—Wilkie Collins, *The Woman in White*

Everything is a cipher and of everything he is the theme.
—Vladimir Nabokov, "Signs and Symbols"

For Joanna

contents

episode three | 145

why i am qualified to write this book

About ten years ago, when I was living in Boston, I had a therapist whose office was in a clinic across the Charles River, at the top of a tall hill. The therapist, whose name was Brian, had a beard and moustache the color of ripe mangoes, and in his spare time he acted in community theater. Often the productions Brian performed in had historical settings, and he would groom his facial hair accordingly. Brian was the best therapist I've ever had, compassionate and patient and wise. But his appearance could be unsettling. One month, as opening night for *The Secret Garden* approached, he trimmed his beard progressively thinner while he grew his moustache thick, extending it down along the sides of his mouth. It was like getting counseling from General Custer.

I had started going to Brian because I was deeply anxious. I'd been so before. This was my third and most serious bout with acute anxiety, and as with the others, my condition seemed disconnected from the facts of my life. I had graduated from college the year before, with honors. I had a prestigious job, loyal friends, a good apartment I shared with a bright and beautiful girlfriend, and as much money as I needed. Yet every day was torture. I slept fitfully, with recurring nightmares: tsunamis, feral animals, the violent deaths of loved ones. I had intestinal cramps and nausea and headaches. A sense of impending catastrophe colored every waking moment. Worse, I had the distinct sense that catastrophe had already occurred. I had made the wrong decisions, gone down the wrong path, screwed up in a ruinous, irrevocable, epoch-making way.

One afternoon, in this state of mind, I walked to therapy. My weekly walks were perilous in that without the distraction of work I was free to berate myself with impunity. There was no need even to concentrate on where I was going—the way to Brian's office lay on the Freedom Trail, a two-and-a-half-mile-long path marked by a painted red line that leads through some of the most famous landmarks of the American Revolution. Boston's beloved Freedom Trail: the Common, the Granary Burying Ground, the Old South Meeting House, the Old North Church, the U.S.S. *Constitution*, . . . Brian's office. It was as if the entire experiment in American democracy was fated to culminate in my recovery.

Anxiety is the most common of psychological complaints, not only the clinical condition that applies to the most people (nearly three of every ten Americans), but, it's often said, a universal and insoluble feature of modern life. Everyone has it; everyone must deal with it. While the corollary to this is that everyone's anxiety is different, shot through with idiosyncratic concerns and confusions, the experience is unified by its painfully hermetic character. Anxiety compels a person to think, but it is the type of thinking that gives thinking a bad name: solipsistic, self-eviscerating, unremitting, vicious. My walks to therapy, for example, were spent outlining with great logical precision the manner in which my state of mind would lead me to complete existential ruin. A typical line of thought went something like this: *I am anxious. The anxiety makes it impossible to concentrate. Because it is impossible to concentrate, I will make an unforgivable mistake at work. Because I will make an unforgivable mistake at work, I will be fired. Because I will be fired, I will not be able to pay my rent. Because I will not be able to pay my rent, I will be forced to have sex for money in an alley behind Fenway Park. Because I will be forced to have sex for money in an alley behind Fenway Park, I will contract HIV. Because I will contract HIV, I will develop full-blown AIDS. Because I will develop full-blown AIDS, I will die disgraced and alone.*

From freeform anxiety to death-by-prostitution in eight short steps. Most weeks, I found that I could kill myself off before I'd crossed the bridge into Charlestown. This gave me a half a mile to fully experience the ignominy of my downfall: to see my mother wailing like a Sicilian peasant over my lime-complected corpse, to see the rabbi eulogizing my unfulfilled promise, to hear the thump of dirt on unfinished pine, to accompany my two brothers as they rush home from graveside to pull the plastic wrap off the cold-cut platters and switch on the coffee urn. Meanwhile, mounting the hill to the clinic, near-horizontal against the angle of ascent, I would do my best to weep—for cathartic purposes. These were pathetic attempts at weeping, the bleaty cries of someone who has wept himself dry, like an ape laughing: "Hunh! Hunh! Hunh!" Sweaty with strain and agitation, I would try to manufacture bona fide tears and always—always—I would fail. By the time I arrived at the clinic I was typically so demoralized I could barely stand. I was twenty-three years old and I looked like Nixon resigning the presidency.

My opening monologues in therapy, like my en route self-destructions, rarely varied. I would open by insisting that I was a thoroughgoing wreck. My anxiety had grown so intense over the preceding week that I could no longer in good faith work. The only honorable thing for me to do was to leave my job. Following that, I would insist that my pain was so acute that it surely signaled legitimate insanity of one stripe or another, and that it would border on malpractice for Brian to continue to see me as an outpatient; what I required was hospitalization, preferably at an institution with manicured grounds and nurses who wore starched white hats with red crosses embroidered on them. Finally, I would plead for help. I would insist that Brian tell me what to do. *Please,* I would say. *Please. Just tell me what to do. I can't do this on my own. I'm not capable. Tell me what I need to do. I'll do anything. Please. I'm begging you. Please. What should I do?*

It was at some point during this opening speech, on the afternoon I am talking about, that Brian interrupted and asked if he could film me. Brian taught graduate students, he explained, and he sometimes used videotaped sessions during his seminars, for training purposes.

"You want to tape me?" I asked.

"For training purposes," he said. "You can say no, of course."

"I can?" I said. "I can say no?"

"Yes, of course."

"It would be all right?"

"Yes."

"You'd still be able to teach?"

"Yes."

"So it's OK?"

"Yes."

"No."

And so we carried on as if he had never made the request. For the forty or so minutes remaining in the session I sat wretched with hopelessness as Brian nodded and made maddeningly benign facial expressions, as was his habit. Then I retraced the steps of Paul Revere and Sam Adams and all the rest of the great patriots, this time in reverse, and returned to the office for the few terrible hours remaining in my professional day.

It was only later, while riding home on the train to hide under the covers until morning, that I realized why Brian had wanted to tape me. It was the same thing that had happened to my brother David, years earlier. When he was in grade school, David had severe buck teeth, broad and walrus-long. His overbite was so pronounced that our orthodontist, when he had finally managed to correct the problem, used a plaster cast of David's teeth as a display during lectures at conferences, as if to say to the world of corrective dentistry, "Behold, people! This is how bad it can get!"

My case, I realized, was Brian's bucktooth mold. I was the clinical example: the etching of the arch-backed epileptic; the lithograph of the withered, birth-defected arm; the tumor with lips and a tongue; the six-eyed, noseless, baguette-shaped head in the jar.

I was anxiety personified.

episode one

If you really feel like you have to write a book, at least have the decency to start it with a man and a woman making love.

—Advice given by my grandfather

1.

genesis

The story begins with two women, naked, in a living room in upstate New York.

In the living room, the blinds have been drawn. The coffee table, which is stained and littered with ashtrays, empty bottles, and a tall blue bong, has been pushed against the far wall. The couch has been unfurled. It is a cheap couch, with no springs or gears or wooden endoskeleton; its cushions unfold flat onto the floor with a flat slapping sound: *thwack*. Also on the floor are several clear plastic bags containing dental dams, spermicidal lubricant, and latex gloves. There is everything, it seems to me, but an oxygen tank and a gurney.

I am hunched in an awkward squat behind a woman on all fours, a woman who is blond and overweight. Her buttocks are exposed and her knees are spread wide—"presenting," they call it in most mammalian species. I am sixteen years old. I have never before seen a vagina up close, an in-person vagina. My prior experience has been limited to two-dimensional vaginas, usually with creases and binding staples marring the view. To mark the occasion, I would like to shake the vagina's hand, talk to it for a while. *How do you do, vagina? Would you like some herbal tea?* But the vagina is businesslike and gruff. An impatient vagina, a waiting vagina. A real bureaucrat of a vagina.

I inch closer on the tips of my toes, knees bent, hands out, fingers splayed—portrait of the writer as a young lecher. The air in the room smells like a combination of a women's locker room and an off-track betting parlor, all smoke and sweat and scented lotions. My condom, the first I've had occasion to wear in anything other than experimental conditions, pinches and dims sensation, so that my penis feels like what I imagine a phantom limb must feel like. The second woman has brown hair done up in curls, round hips, and dark, biscuit-wide nipples. She lies on the couch, waiting. As I proceed, foot by foot, struggling to keep my erection and my balance at the same time, her eyes coax me forward. She is touching herself.

Now the target vagina is only a foot away. Now I feel like a military plane, preparing for in-air refueling. I feel, also, like a symbol. This is why I am here, ultimately. This is why, when the invitation was extended ("Do you want to stay? I want you to stay"), I accepted, and waited who knows how long in the dark room for them to return. How could I have said no? What I had been offered was every boy's dream. Two women. The dream.

Through a haze of cannabis and cheap beer, I bolster my courage with this: the dream. What I am about to do is not for myself. It is for my people, my tribe. *Dear friends, this is not my achievement. This is* your *achievement. Your* victory. *A fulfillment of your desires. Oh poor, suffering, groin-sore boys of the eleventh grade, I hereby dedicate this vagina to—*

It is then that the woman coughs. It is a rattling, hacking

cough. A cough of nicotine and phlegm. And the vagina, which is connected to the cough's apparatus by some internal musculature I could not possibly have imagined before this moment, winks at me. With its wild, bushy, thorny lashes, it winks. My heart flutters. My breathing quickens. I have been winked at by a vagina that looks like Andy Rooney. I feel a tightness in my chest and I think to myself, *Oh dear lord, what have I gotten myself into?*

2.

hurricane marilyn

I'll call her Esther. The plump blonde with the unkempt pubic hair and the penchant for teenage boys. The penchant for me. I met her while working at a bookstore in Plainview, New York, at the rough longitudinal and latitudinal center of Long Island, where I was born and raised. She took an instant liking to me and then she took my virginity, and going on two decades later my mind still hasn't recovered. Esther set my anxiety off. She was the match that lit the psychic fire. It all starts with Esther.

Either that or it starts with my mother. I can never decide. Losing my virginity in a way that even my most depraved friends find unfortunate had an immediate and profound impact on me. But my mother set up the circumstance whereby there could be a trigger like Esther, whereby it was only a matter of time until something set me off. In every important way—cognitive, behavioral, environmental, genetic—my mother laid the foundation of this intractable problem of mine.

(This is no recovery memoir, let me warn you now.)

• • •

Months ago, when I told my mother I was writing a book about anxiety, she said, "A book about anxiety? But that was *my* idea. I had that idea. Sheila"—her close friend of many years—"and I were going to do it together. Then she dropped dead, so we didn't. But we talked about it for years. That's not fair!"

I didn't know what she meant wasn't fair: my writing a book she wanted to write, Sheila dropping dead, or both. I pointed out that writing about anxiety was not an original idea. Freud wrote a book about anxiety ninety years ago. Kierkegaard wrote one eighty years before that. Spinoza wrote one in the eighteenth century. In any case, I hadn't known she wanted to write a book about anxiety, or about anything for that matter.

"We should do it together!" she said. "We could coauthor. A mother-son book about anxiety? People would eat it up. We'd make a fortune!"

I replied that it was an interesting thought but that it probably wouldn't work. I'd never written with anyone before. I had trouble writing if a person's photograph was in the room with me. How would I tolerate a living human being?

Later, before we hugged good-bye, I asked my mother if she would mind if I wrote about her. She didn't hesitate a moment. "I don't give a shit. I'm old! I'm tired! I work too much!"

The first of these three claims is relative, the second hard to believe. In her late sixties, my mother has more energy than most college students I've met. She has more energy than most squirrels I've met. My brother Scott and I have a nickname for my mother: "Hurricane Marilyn." We use the nickname when we catch sight of her climbing out of her car just before a visit to one of our homes. We watch her cross the street, arms flailing, keys and receipts and gifts for the grandchildren spilling from multiple bags, a fast-moving storm front of narration and complaint and anecdote and fervent family affection—a Jewish mother, in short, of the first order—and we shout, "Batten the hatches, everyone! Hurricane Marilyn's about to make landfall!"

My mother's third claim, however, is true. When my father died, in the late 1990s, of cancer, he didn't leave much money, and it's unlikely my mother will ever be in a position to retire. She complains about this, but the truth is she loves her work. She takes pride in her talent and her experience, and in the value she adds to the world. For here is the most telling fact about my mother's contribution to my psychological life: She is a psychotherapist. She treats all sorts of people with all sorts of complaints. But she specializes in the anxiety disorders.

Like most clichés, it is fundamentally true that the anxious, the melancholy, the manic, and the obsessed are more likely to become therapists than other people. Before she was a therapist, my mother was a sufferer and a patient. She is still a patient, but she claims not to be much of a sufferer anymore. My mother portrays herself as an anxiety success story, a living example of how will, wisdom, and clinical psychology can triumph over nature.

It is a rough nature. To hear my mother tell it, her teens, twenties, and thirties consisted of an almost unbroken chain of hundreds of full-blown panic attacks—a riot of flop sweats, hyperventilation, and self-reproach. Her nerves were so exquisitely sensitive to stimuli that in order to dull them she would sneak shots of vodka before walking to school in the morning. She was scared of driving, public speaking, parties, open spaces, and men. She experienced feelings of unreality and dizziness. She suffered from acid indigestion, heart palpitations, and tremors. She had panic attacks at school. She also had panic attacks at home, at the grocery store, at the laundromat, at the bank, in the shower, and in bed. She had a panic attack when my father came to her work to propose to her. "My hands shook," she had told me. "The thought of having to stay still while someone put a ring on my finger made me nuts!"

Recently, I asked my mother how this all ended. How had she gotten to the point where she no longer experienced the world as one giant firecracker at her back? She answered with a story.

When she was around forty, my mother said, she had a therapist who worked at a renowned clinic for people with phobias, a clinic that was attached to a large private hospital. The therapist was impressed by my mother's intelligence and pluck; she felt that my mother possessed a strength that, unlike many other people prone to panic, compelled her to do things in spite of her fear of them. She asked, not entirely ethically, if my mother would like to come work for her at the clinic. My mother's job would involve leading groups of phobics out into the world to expose them to situations that typically made them hysterical with fear. She would be the blind leading the blind, therapeutically.

The first people my mother took out were four elderly patients afraid, in various combinations, of driving, shopping, and generally being among other people. My mother was still afraid of these things, too, particularly driving. She decided to take them to a nearby shopping center. She drove them in her own car. At first things didn't go badly. No one passed out, no one threw up, no one ran screaming into the parking lot. Then, on the way back to the clinic, the car broke down. This was before cell phones. They were on the narrow shoulder of a busy four-lane road. The cars hurtled past, making unnerving Doppler noises. Everyone's blood pressure started to rise. Everyone started to pant just a little. What happens when five clinically anxious people have a simultaneous panic attack in a 1983 Buick LeSabre? My mother didn't want to find out.

She tried to flag down a cab. No one would stop. The drivers took one look at the passengers—all that papery skin, all those wild, rheumy eyes—and pressed down on their accelerators. Now my mother was starting to spin out of control, her mind devising catastrophic tableaus: in police stations, in hospitals, in morgues, local television crews filming the whole thing. She started to shake and sweat and enter a kind of waking nightmare state.

Just then a cab stopped at a red light. My mother hustled the old folks to the corner, flung open the back door, and over the driver's angry objections shoved them inside. It was only when the light turned green and the driver was forced to submit that my mother saw why he'd been reluctant to take them in. It wasn't just that they looked like cornered animals or that they had basically commandeered his vehicle. It was that he already had a passenger and that passenger was—I've made my mother swear to this fact—a pregnant woman in labor. The driver dropped the woman off first.

This is not what I thought my mother would say when I asked how she had conquered the worst of her anxiety. I thought she would say something like, "I worked hard, with the help of medication, targeted psychotherapy, vigorous exercise, the support of your father and friends, and various meditative, yogic, and muscle-relaxation techniques, to change the way my mind operates." All of which is true. To my surprise, however, what helped my mother first and foremost wasn't a conscious, critical analysis or counterbalancing of her fears, but tossing herself—and in this case being tossed—into direct confrontation with the very things that most terrified her.

Clinical psychology has a term for this sort of approach. It is "flooding." The first patient on whom flooding was used successfully, in the 1950s, was an adolescent girl who suffered from a paralyzing fear of cars. "She was kept compulsorily in the back of a car in which she was continuously driven for four hours," reads one description of the treatment. "Her fear soon reached panic proportions, and then gradually subsided. At the end of the ride she was quite comfortable, and henceforth was free from phobia."

This is a chilling passage, especially that "compulsorily." How did they compel her, one wonders? Did orderlies hold her down? Did they remove the door handles? In four hours you can drive from Midtown Manhattan to the Washington Monument, if you don't stop for gas.

My mother's afternoon with her four elderly phobics was a kind of informal flooding treatment. What greater terror for a woman afraid of losing control than an outing in which she is the authority and control doesn't hold? All the world conspired to make her panic. Yet she didn't. She couldn't. If she panicked, the situation would have disintegrated. Equally as therapeutic was the fact that disaster did not come. Returning her wards safely to the clinic, arranging for a tow truck, and making it home that evening was like a gradual waking from a dream in which she had been pursued and mauled by wolves—and was fine. She scanned herself. No bites? No scratches? No wounds? It had all been in her head.

So began my mother's career as a therapist, a flooding cure slower yet more radical than anything even the most reptilian of behaviorists might prescribe. In the kingdom of the anxious, those with simple phobias have it easy. If you're afraid of heights, lean over a railing. If you're afraid of germs, lick a floor. But what do you do if your greatest fear is of being afraid? This was the essence of my mother's predicament. She had been diagnosed with "panic disorder," a condition that comes down to this: panicking about panicking. You have one panic attack and it leaves you uneasy, vigilant for another. You search for threats to your stability and, because this is life, you find them, and have another panic attack. That attack makes you more vigilant, which leads to more attacks, which leads to more vigilance, and so on and so forth until your mental existence is as cramped and airless as a broom closet. There are ways to break out—the world is stuffed with theories on how to escape anxiety—but none as extreme as the one my mother chose.

3.

monkey mind

I was nine when my mother went back to school to become a therapist and twelve when she graduated. For most of my life she had worked as a teacher, first in the public schools, then as the codirector of a day care that operated out of a neighbor's basement. Now she bought an ad in the *Pennysaver* and began to see patients at home, in a large, low-ceilinged room on the bottom floor of our house. For her children, this meant a slew of new rules and obligations.

Rule one was silence—or as close an approximation of silence as three pubescent boys could manage. When my mother was in session with a patient, we were forbidden to stomp, shout, wrestle, fight, or anything else that, in a moderately sized suburban house, might resonate through the drywall, which was basically everything except reading or muted self-abuse. There was a cracked cement path leading to the patients' entrance, in the back of the house. In the fall, we had to rake the leaves from the path; in the winter, we had to sprinkle rock salt on it; in the spring and summer, we had to water the rose bushes in the flower beds beside it. We had to do these things far in advance of a patient's arrival. My mother didn't want some trembling neurotic startled witless by the sight of a shirtless boy wielding a spray gun. For the same reason, it was firmly suggested that we stay indoors throughout all fifty-minute hours. My mother's office had a long window that looked out onto our backyard. The therapeutic couch (overstuffed leather, beige) faced in the opposite direction, but there was always the chance that a client would look over his shoulder, with unpredictable clinical results. Say my mother was treating a man whose wife had taken the kids and left. How would he react to seeing my brother and me idyllically tossing around a football?

So we stayed out of sight and out of earshot. It was the new domestic order, and it stung like exile. Before my mother hung her diploma on the wall and laid in a supply of tissues, the room that became her office hadn't been vacant. It had been the den, the sweetly dim, subterranean place, wall-to-wall carpeted, where we watched movies and played Battleship and rode out bouts of chicken pox and the flu. It was the cultural and recreational soul of our house, and its sudden transformation made me feel the way Parisians must have felt when the Nazis invaded and took all the good tables at the cafés.

One of the places to which I retreated after my mother changed careers was my parents' bedroom, directly above the purloined den, where there was a large TV, a queen-sized bed, and a wealth of thick down pillows. As it turned out, there was something revelatory there as well, something that would start me wondering, hazily at first, about my mother's mind and its influence on my own. I made the discovery by accident one evening when, yawning, I knocked the TV remote off the bed. I looked for it the way kids look for fallen remotes: upside-down, hanging off the mattress, bent at the waist like a hinge. That's when I heard it. In the dusty gap between the bed and my father's nightstand there was a corrugated central-air vent, and coming from the vent was the sound of voices:

WOMAN (HUSKY-VOICED, FORTIES OR FIFTIES): . . . like it's going to collapse. Like it's just going to cave in. Like it's going to cave right the hell in. Steel beams, wire cables, asphalt, road signs, cars, trucks, steamrollers. Whatever. The whole thing. The whole fucking thing just collapsing right into the goddamn Sound.

MY MOTHER: How often do you have to drive across it?

WOMAN: Twice a week! Twice a week across a bridge that looks like it was built during the fucking Depression! I could kill myself. . . . Not really. I'm just kidding. You know that, right?

MY MOTHER: Mm-hm.

WOMAN: I don't have the balls to kill myself.

MY MOTHER: Mm-hm.

WOMAN: If only I did, I could avoid that commute. . . . God! It's the look of those bolts that really rips my heart out. Those whaddya call 'em—rivets? The things that hold the I beams together?

MY MOTHER: . . .

WOMAN: They look *rusty.* Like they could just snap at any minute. Like they could just buckle and snap and then that's it. Game over! End of story! Down we all go! And probably we're not even dead before we splash down. How long does it take to fall, what, a hundred feet? Two hundred? Do we die on impact? Do we die of hypothermia? Do we drown? How long does it take to drown?

MY MOTHER: . . .

WOMAN: I'm actually asking. Do you know how long it takes to drown?

MY MOTHER: No.

WOMAN: Well, I die. That's all I know.

MY MOTHER: . . .

WOMAN: . . .

MY MOTHER: And what frightens you?

WOMAN: Are you kidding me? Haven't you been listening? Plummeting to my death! That's what frightens me.

MY MOTHER: . . .

WOMAN: Isn't that enough?

MY MOTHER: Well, there are several parts to what you're telling me. To the scenario. There's the thought that the bridge will collapse, there's the act of falling, and there's the actual dying. Which part makes you anxious?

WOMAN: All of them.

MY MOTHER: . . .

WOMAN. The dying.

MY MOTHER: Why?

WOMAN: Because of R_____.

MY MOTHER: What about her?

WOMAN: What'll she do without me? Who'll take care of her?

MY MOTHER: How about her husband?

WOMAN: Her husband! Her husband can't even make an omelet.

I found the remote a couple of minutes into this exchange, resting against my father's slippers, and turned off the TV. This was far more interesting than *Matlock*. Now I can see it as fairly unremarkable stuff: A middle-aged woman with a bridge phobia is hardly therapeutic dynamite. But, then, it wasn't the patient who for the next half hour kept me dangling from the bed in a state of rapt fascination. It was my mother. Or rather, I should say, it was the impostor who had taken my mother's voice. For what entranced me was the sense that I had inadvertently gained access to an identity radically out of joint with the one I knew. The mother I knew was the impulsive, uncontainable one I've described, a Bronx-born grocer's daughter with a hug like a carpenter's vise. The one drifting up through the vent was, by comparison, a Zen master: cool, circumspect, mindful. That my mother could placate suffering came as no surprise. She was my mother; she'd been placating my suffering since the maternity ward. But that she could do it logically and dispassionately; that her soothing could come from a place of reason rather than from her guts; that she could *choreograph* her healing, restrain it, direct it, mete it out with deliberation—these were stunners. These were the revelations that drew me back to the vent day after day, week after week, spying on the sacrosanct with blood pooling in my ears.

A couple of years ago, I paid a visit to Scott, my oldest brother, to talk about anxiety. This wasn't an unusual topic. Scott and I talk about anxiety the way some brothers talk about money, which is to say often, and always with an eye on who has more of it. In truth, however, we aren't in competition. Our anxieties are different breeds. Mine is cerebral. It starts with a thought—a *what if* or a *should have been* or a *never will be* or a *could have been*—and metastasizes from there, sparking down the spine and rooting out into the body in the form of breathlessness, clamminess, fatigue, palpitations, and a terrible sense that the world in which I find myself is at once holographically unsubstantial and grotesquely threatening.

Scott's anxiety is more physical. It starts with a twinge or an unaccustomed tightness and then rises to his mind, which, in the natural process of investigating the sensation, magnifies it, which results in further investigation, which further magnifies the sensation, creating a feedback loop that ends with Scott either curled up on the couch with a jar of Nutella and a sack of soy crisps or strapped to a gurney in an ambulance, being rushed to the cardiac unit for a battery of tests that invariably reveals nothing more malignant than a few gas bubbles. In short, Scott is a hypochondriac.

Scott and I sometimes argue about the relative demerits of my "free-floating" versus his "somatic" anxiety. But mainly we commiserate. We whine, we exchange strategies for how to settle ourselves down, and we test out pet theories on each other. On this visit, I wanted to talk to Scott about my anxiety's origins.

We talked in Scott's kitchen. He was starting dinner for his family, scraping minced garlic and onions into a cast-iron skillet. I told Scott about my theory that the onset of my anxiety coincided with the moment I lost my virginity. That was the turn, the evolutionary, or devolutionary, leap. Before: normal childhood. After: quaking adulthood. The smell of sautéing aromatics is a kind of natural sedative, an air-borne Valium. It loosens the tongue. I spoke for a long while. When I was finished, Scott gave the pan an expert little toss and said, in the tone professors use with their least perceptive students, "Jesus, Dan. Maybe. I guess. But listen: It's not like we were raised by Buddhist monks."

There are two things to say about this statement. First, contrary to popular belief, Buddhists can actually be very anxious people. That's often why they become Buddhists in the first place. Buddhism was made for the anxious like Christianity was made for the downtrodden or AA for the addicted. Its entire purpose is to foster equanimity, to tame excesses of thought and emotion. The Buddhists have a great term for these excesses. They refer to them as the condition of "monkey mind." A person in the throes of monkey mind suffers from a consciousness whose constituent parts will not stop bouncing from skull-side to skull-side, which keep flipping and jumping and flinging feces at the walls and swinging from loose neurons like howlers from vines. Buddhist practices are designed explicitly to collar these monkeys of the mind and bring them down to earth—to pacify them. Is it any wonder that Buddhism has had such tremendous success in the bastions of American nervousness, on the West Coast and in the New York metro area?

The second thing to say about Scott's admonition is that I'd never before realized how influential our upbringing must have been. It seems remarkable, because he's right. Of course he's right. An account of my anxiety that vaulted over my mother's was like starting *Moby-Dick* when the whale takes a harpoon in the flank. And not just my mother's anxiety. Scott spoke in the plural: monks, not monk. We were raised by two anxious parents. My father's anxiety was as different from my mother's anxiety as Scott's is different from mine, darker and more complicated. But it was there, sometimes in force. In his early forties, my father had a series of panic attacks that literally laid him flat, and then sent him packing to the behavioral ward for a rest. Meanwhile, all the while, my mother was struggling to make it through PTA meetings without hyperventilating herself into unconsciousness. And still I didn't realize.

Did I have intimations? A year into my mother's clinical career I sneaked into her office and defaced the first few business cards she kept in a pale porcelain dispenser on her desk. The cards, of which she was very proud, read:

MARILYN SMITH, MSW
PSYCHOTHERAPIST

When I was through they read:

MARILYN SMITH
PSYCHO

But this was an act more of mischief than of understanding. I had no real knowledge that my mother's therapeutic work grew out of her therapeutic needs. I had no real knowledge that she *had* therapeutic needs, that there was anything to her temperament but her: the maternal constant. Anxiety has many signs: ragged nails, gnawed cuticles, sweaty palms, excessive blinking, the inability to sit still for more than a moment. All the things the monkey does when he's in command. But you have to know what to look for. And even if you know you may not find anything. The more practiced anxiety sufferers are adept at the art of subterfuge. For the sake of propriety, ambition, desire, or privacy, they learn to seal their anxiety off from public view. They learn to cork their anxiety within themselves like acid in a vial. It isn't pleasant. The human mind isn't Pyrex; it can corrode. But it works.

But a child is a sensitive instrument. You can hide the factual truth from a child, but you can't blanket influence. Your agitation will out, and over time it will mold your child's temperament as surely as water wears at rock. It was not until I was nearly twenty, deep into my own way with anxiety, that my mother spoke to me explicitly about her anxiety and the grief it caused her. But by that time she was essentially talking to herself. I'd become her. It wasn't merely genetics. It was the million little signals: the jolting movements, the curious fears, the subtle avoidances, the panic behind the eyes, the terror behind the hugs, the tremor in the caresses. It was the monkey. A child registers who's raising him.

After I went to talk to Scott, I went to visit my mother in her office. It isn't the office I knew as a child. A few years after my father died my mother sold the house and moved to a condo development farther east on Long Island. She now sees patients in a single-story suite dominated by a chiropractic office. Between patients, she sometimes pops next door for a lumbar adjustment.

My mother and I are close and usually easy with each other. Yet from the moment we sat down she bobbed her legs and squirmed. She was sitting on her sturdy clinician's chair. I was on the clients' couch, beneath a print of Andrew Wyeth's *Christina's World*—a girl lying on a parched, sloping field. When the phone rang, my mother answered, "I can't talk now, Donna. I'm being tortured by Daniel." Then, hanging up: "I'm nervous!"

"Why?" I asked. "Why are you nervous?"

"I'm nervous," she said, "because I don't want to fuck up your book."

"You won't fuck up my book, Mom. How could you? It hasn't even happened yet."

"Exactly. The book hasn't happened yet. That's what I'm afraid about."

"And anyway, the whole concept is that—"

"Concept!" She spat the word out like it was a bad olive. "That's just the beginning, the concept. You've got to put it into words. And I'm nervous. I have anticipatory anxiety."

"You have anticipatory anxiety because you think if the interview goes poorly the book might not come out well?"

"I'm nervous because . . . because I'm the queen of anxiety and you're the prince, and if the interview goes poorly, and it's my fault, then yeah, the book might not go as well."

The Queen and the Prince. She'd never put it like that before. It might have sounded prideful if it hadn't been so thickly larded with guilt. What my mother was feeling, it soon emerged, was responsible—for everything. I'd come to ask a few simple questions and she reacted as if I'd brought along klieg lights and a set of dental instruments.

"I'm sorry!" she said. "I fucked up. I'm sorry. I did! I didn't know how to raise kids. I was anxious. And I was naïve. I thought we'd get it right by the time you came along. You were number three. Raising kids was supposed to be like making pancakes. The first couple always come out a little mangled, but by the third everything's usually pretty smooth. But I got in my own way. I was anxious. I'm so sorry."

I felt awful to have made her feel awful. At seventeen, perhaps, I would have savored my mother's remorse. At double the age, any blame I ascribe to her anxiety is overwhelmed by admiration for what she's done with it. For thirty years, my mother's anxiety disallowed her the comfort, easy amiability, and confidence she believed she detected in her peers. It lined her mind with garish mirrors. I know what the nervous system hungers for under these conditions. It hungers for unconsciousness—or, failing that, inebriation of one kind or another. Like all anxious people, my mother engaged in her fair share of escapism. Unlike many, however, she didn't narcotize her way out of anxiety. Nor did she take the other popular path, that of lifelong miserable resignation. Instead, she stood and did battle.

She didn't win; no one wins. It was more like she struck a bargain. The bargain was this: Admit the anxiety as an essential part of yourself and in exchange that anxiety will be converted into energy, unstable but manageable. Stop with the self-flagellating and become yourself, with scars and tics. That my brothers and I at times judge this bargain harshly—that we see it, sometimes, as a stubborn unwillingness to exert maximal control—is in the logic of my mother's life beside the point. My mother took the measure of what could be built with the material she'd been given, and she built it. More than that, she has built shelter for others, hundreds of others. It's no insignificant thing. Anxiety is a selfishness machine. To have found a way to use it for good is unusual indeed. Long live the Queen.

A couple of weeks after I visited my mother's office, my cell phone vibrated and lit up and the following text message appeared:

> From: Mom
> just drove by stonybrook pond where you almost
> drowned! start of anxiety? xoxoxo
> CB: 516-606-XXXX

I had forgotten all about this, which is strange because it's an oft-told tale—Family Story #289. It refers to an event that occurred in the fall of 1980, when I was three. The setting was

Mill Pond, in Stony Brook's T. Bayles Minuse Park, on the North
Shore. The occasion was an outing with the extended family: my
parents, my aunt and uncle, my brothers, my two cousins, and
me. The genre of the story—at least as it has been told in the
family ever since—is comedy.

The first part of the story is simple to tell: I wandered away
from the group and fell into the pond. Mill Pond is filled with
ducks and massive, ill-tempered swans, who steal the bread that
children feed to the ducks. The pond has no gate or railing along
its perimeter. It's just grass, then dirt, then a ragged stone lip,
then water. I was a toddler; I was toddling. I don't know what
everyone else was doing. My brothers and older cousin were no
doubt running around, laughing and arguing. The adults were no
doubt sitting around, laughing and arguing. In any event, no one
was paying attention, and no one remembers exactly how long the
heedlessness lasted. It could have been a minute, it could have
been five, it could have been more. By the time someone thought
to check on me, I was face down among the fowl—arms at my
sides, motionless. Someone screamed, my mother screamed in
turn, and she sprinted to the pond.

So far, so unfunny. It doesn't take long for a child to asphyxi-
ate. Short of death there is the risk of brain damage. Time is
of the essence. It is this, coupled with the fact that I emerged
physically unharmed, that has led my mother to have to take a
decades-long ribbing about what happened next. At the time my
mother was a serious amateur photographer, and as she rushed
to the pond she had hanging from her neck a brand-new, 1980
Winter Olympics collectors' edition, Canon AE-1 camera with
a focal plane shutter and an interchangeable lens. There are two
versions of what she did with this camera once she reached the
pond. One version has it that, leaping without hesitation into the

water, she held her camera far aloft with one hand while with the other she scooped me up and carried me to safety. The other version—uncharacteristic, but who knows?—has my mother actually pausing at the bank of the pond to remove the camera from her neck and place it on the ground before coming to my rescue. Whatever the truth, the point of the story is that right there at the water's edge my mother performed a sort of farcical reenactment of *Sophie's Choice,* the main difference from the original being that instead of having to choose between the lives of her two children, my mother had to choose between her child and a piece of luxury electronics.

To be fair to my mother, who now refers to Mill Pond as "the place where I was horribly negligent and almost let my three-year-old drown," the Canon AE-1 is a fine camera. She still has it. After being pulled from the water, however, I wouldn't, or couldn't, say a word. A bystander at the pond offered a quilt and my mother bundled me up and took me to my aunt's house, where she held me in front of the fire, rocking me and berating herself. For the next eighteen hours I was mute.

When I woke the next morning I was my usual garrulous, playful, enervating self, as if nothing had happened. Near-death experience? Who wants to build a fort? Post-traumatic stress? Let's watch *Sesame Street*!

Yet when my mother's text came in I knew immediately what she meant. This is the trouble with origin hunting: There are so many origins. My mother may blame her genes and her temperament for my anxiety, but as a therapist she believes firmly in the transformative power of adversity—the ability of negative emotions to startle awake the devils in our chromosomes. Finding traumas is her business the same way that finding the murderer is the detective's business. It's what she is trained to do, and it is the skill that, after our conversation, she applied vigorously to my case. She went looking in my past for clues, and merely by mentioning the pond incident I knew the clues she had found. They were the episodes of my childhood fear of water.

Clue #1: The September following my near drowning, I am outside with my brothers. Our house is one of four in a small horseshoe-shaped cul-de-sac where the neighborhood children like to play. Suddenly my mother hears a high-pitched, operatic wail, a panicked air-siren of a scream. She rushes outside to find me wide-mouthed and shivering, my fists at my temples and, at my feet—at everyone's feet—a half inch of rising water. A neighbor, it seems, has decided to empty his swimming pool into the street and the minor deluge has set me off into some post-traumatic flashback. My mother thinks of this now as my first panic attack.

Clue #2: The following year I become fervently afraid of the toilet. Abruptly, I lose all confidence that the act of flushing away my excretions will work as it always has. Rather than causing everything to sink down the pipes and into the septic system, pushing the toilet's handle will, I become convinced, cause everything to rise up—a physics-defying, endless rising up. It isn't the filth that terrifies me; it is the water. The toilet will overflow and the water will creep steadily up the walls, eventually pushing open the bathroom door, cascading down the carpeted staircase in a foaming torrent, and filling the house like a fishbowl. And I will drown.

Clue #3: Two years pass and I develop a fear of swimming. Won't go near a pool. Won't look at one. Can't even catch a whiff of chlorine without hyperventilating. Hoping to clip this fear at its bud, my parents sign me up for swimming lessons. The first and only lesson takes place at an indoor pool with mosaic-tile walls and a vaulted ceiling, the kind of place in which every sound above the smallest whisper is amplified and echoed many times over. The sounds I begin to make as my father leads me to the pool are way above whispers, and are filled with obscenities so ornate and vulgar that under different circumstances he might have taken some pride in my precocious mastery of them. Under these circumstances, he is preoccupied with simultaneously holding fast to me while not allowing my nails to catch his skin and draw blood. Squirming free, I bolt to the locker room and wrap my thin arms around a changing bench until my father relents and takes me home.

Clue #4: At around the same time, my mother tries to transition me from chewable to swallowable daily vitamins. Although I have no trouble eating and drinking normally, I endure months of embarrassing failures before I successfully make the switch. It's perplexing. I appear to have some psychological block against swallowing pills. My throat closes, I gag, and out the tablet soars, arcing across the kitchen before skidding to a stop on the table or floor, or else cleaving momentarily to the white linoleum cabinets, then falling with a moist clack to the countertop. It isn't the vitamin, it emerges under parental questioning, that causes everything to clench. It's the water or juice or milk or soda. The fluid passing my lips is the sensation that trips the warning system within me. The pills are tiny. Even if one were to get lodged in my trachea I'd be able to breathe comfortably. But the fluid—the fluid could choke me dead.

Could be, I suppose. It's a theory. But like many theories, it's selective. It feeds off cherry-picked evidence. I was a hydrophobic, yes, but I was hypersensitive and neurotic in other ways, too. There are many flavors of anxiety. My childhood was a taster's menu.

I would gladly skip over the mundane examples—your run-of-the-mill fears of the dark, ghosts, the basement, the attic, the woods, animals, doctors, old people, solitude, separation—were it not for the fact that even these anxieties manifested themselves in me with gusto. Among my strongest memories of childhood are of being physically restrained by medical personnel. It was not unusual, when I was young, for a procedure as routine and non-invasive as a strep culture to set me off like a pig in a barn fire. It often required as many as four grown men, one for each scrawny, thrashing limb, to pin me down while a fifth drove home the inoculation or swabbed my swollen tonsils. I can still remember the look that invariably came over the doctor's face as I began to claw at the clinic door and throw fistfuls of tongue depressors at him. It was the same expression the priest in *The Exorcist* wears when Linda Blair spouts pea soup on his frock.

Sometimes grown-ups were conscripted not to restrain me but to pry me loose from wherever I had affixed myself. Like a tick, I was forever clinging to things for survival. My mother still questions whether she and my father were right to leave me at summer camp when, halfway through a mere two-week inaugural stint, they paid a visit and I reacted as if I'd been held hostage by the Iranians and negotiations had just broken down. When they tried to leave, the counselors had to wrench me from the backseat of their car by my ankles.

I don't know how long it was after that that the compulsions started, but I know they threatened to lift my anxiety to a new level of self-consciousness. What but some defect itself compels a child to run his index finger over the total surface area of a dinner plate before his anxiety subsides, or to flick the lights on and off precisely twelve times before leaving a room, or to count the underside of his teeth with his tongue by twos? What but something wrong, something fundamentally *off*, compels a child to clear his throat fifty times a minute, convinced that there is a minuscule but unnervingly sensible blemish in there, a freckle or fold or wrinkle or mole, that only coughing will smooth over?

I didn't know. That's the point. Deep into adolescence I didn't know. To pursue the matter would have been premature. Who cared, in the end, about my breaststroke, so long as I was otherwise active? Who cared about coughing so long as it didn't signal actual ill health? Who cared about anxiety, even, so long as there was still a chance it wouldn't flash the full length of its fangs? Even then it was possible that I wouldn't become my mother.

Then Esther stepped into my life.

4.

esther

She came jangling into the bookstore out of the literal suburban blue, wearing a fulsome smile and looking like a Midwestern diner waitress in a gingham dress and white tennis shoes. Esther's presence in that place, at that time in her life, baffled me from the start. According to her job application she was in her twenties, a recent college graduate with an impressive academic record. She presented herself as well read, worldly, and ambitious. She wasn't what you would call pretty. She was small-headed and thick, not fat but abundant, fleshy beyond an ideal one could not help but imagine for her. Her nose was piggish and her teeth too small. But she was provocative. She carried herself with panache, flaunting her curves with low-cut blouses and thin, clinging fabrics. She was lively and chatty and stuffed with ideas, and all this made her seem out of place. By all convention Esther should have been in Manhattan or San Francisco or Los Angeles, rather than where she was, which was at the rump end of a strip mall midway along the Port Jefferson line of the Long Island Rail Road.

When Esther arrived I was fifteen, and I'd already been working at the bookstore for a year. It is not just because of her that I suspect my mind would be much healthier today if I'd somehow managed to halt my professional development just prior to that employment. I didn't need the work. I already had a job at Food-town, the cavernous, nipple-puckeringly cold supermarket at the opposite end of the strip mall. It was my first job. I worked as what is known as a "leveler."

Levelers, for those unfamiliar with the term, are essentially debris clearers. They are the mass-retail equivalent of the stretcher bearers and ragpickers who would descend onto Civil War battlefields whenever there was a break in the carnage. After the housewife has picked through the yogurt cartons, searching for the freshest date; after the father has palpated the potato chip bags, deluded that any one is fuller than another; after the nanny has shoved aside the chicken broth up front, hoping to find a can with a lower price buried deep within the shelf . . . that's when the leveler springs to work. He gathers the toppled merchandise; he rearranges the items in a neat stack, side by side, one on top of the other; he rotates them so that their bright labels face front. Then he waits, Sisyphus-like, for it all to happen again. Leveling is a repetitive, mindless, benumbing job, and it is only now, far too late, that I see how perfect it was for a person of my temperament. My father was a lawyer, and he used to half-joke that he should have become a housepainter instead. What he meant was that unlike lawyering, housepainting has soothingly clear and finite ends. Leveling is like that. There is never any confusion. There is never any ambiguity. There is just the discrete and achievable task, forever.

That I didn't stay a leveler I blame on a book. In the ninth grade we were assigned *Of Mice and Men* and, self-sequestered in my grandmother's bedroom in the moments before a Rosh

Hashanah dinner, hunched with my back against her closet door, I read the famous climax, in which George, trembling with antici-pated grief and regret, shoots big, dumb, rabbit-obsessed Lennie in the back of the head—*blam!*—murdering his best friend out of mercy. And for the first time in my reading life I wept. I wept for Lennie. I wept for George. I wept for the plight of itinerant ranchers in prewar northern California. I wept for humanity! When I emerged, red-nostriled and stinking of mothballs, I was in my heart no longer a leveler. After that, whenever I stood outside Foodtown after my shift, I would stare at the bookstore at the other end of the parking lot—past the deli and the drugstore and the framing shop and the stationer's—as if it were some mirage, an oasis of literary sophistication.

It wasn't. As the only game in town besides the library, the store attracted whatever bookish types happened to live in the area—solitary men and women who lingered broodingly in the poetry stacks for full afternoons. But the vast bulk of the store's trade in books was off the best seller rack: the newest Grisham or Koontz or mass-market spiritual phenomenon. And the bulk of the store's trade in general, it turned out, was off the comic-book rack. As much if not more than a bookshop, the store served as a kind of public square for dermatologically afflicted adolescents to congregate and compare notes on the anarchic universe of superheroes, atomic mutants, and demonic villains. They came in droves, these comic-book geeks, day after day, year after year, and in time a large number of them had made their way onto the pay-roll. By the time I started they were part of the inextricable DNA of the place. The store had philosophy. The store had history. The store had leather-bound first editions of nineteenth-century novels. But more than anything else the store was a boy's club, as cliquish, restrictive, and leery of outsiders as the Vatican.

It was under these social conditions that Esther and I became friends. To be more precise: It was under these conditions that Esther chose to befriend me. She didn't have many options. The staff, almost without exception (she was the only female employee), abhorred Esther. They thought her pushy, intrusive, untrustworthy, bizarre—the whole xenophobic litany. Pushy she indisputably was. Esther had the habit of ambushing customers as soon as they entered the store, so that she could steer them toward and sell them on her favorite books. When we ate lunch she would hover at our elbows, waiting for the moment we dabbed our lips to ask, "Mind if I have the rest of that?" If someone teased her about this she would plead shameless poverty, but the staff concluded that she was simply lazy—the type of person who grows fat on other people's food. Then, perhaps most unnerving of all, there was the oddity and incongruity of Esther's love life. She was married, to a slight, quiet young man she paraded into the store one morning. And yet she claimed, early on and often, that she was a lesbian. "I love my husband," she would say. "We have a lot in common. But I only married him because I want a baby. I want to be a mommy."

I was as unsettled by Esther as anyone, maybe more so. Later it would be Esther who would call forth the most powerful, private, physical symptom of my anxiety: a stab of sharp cold in the heart-side of my sternum, as if an icicle had been lodged there. I can remember now feeling the ghost of that sensation whenever she approached me in the store. A blossoming of frost. An inward recoiling. Yet of all the employees who must have had some version of this experience as far as Esther was concerned, I was the only one who didn't reject her. I was the only one who made gestures of acceptance and goodwill, the only one who made her feel as if I liked her and was interested in what she had to say—even though I didn't and wasn't. Of a dozen people, I was the only one who acted charitably toward Esther. In doing so I opened myself up to her friendship and gratitude.

It was not a mistake to be kind to Esther, though for many years I was bitterly convinced it was. Esther made a fair show of ignoring the fact that she was shut out of the store's camaraderie; she never for a moment let on that she knew she was disliked. But of course she did know, and the knowledge of her knowledge, coupled with her inexhaustible ability to act as if she fit in, gave off an odor of terrible sadness. Esther needed a friend. That I was the one who volunteered for the position has nonetheless always been a source of great confusion for me. Given all that shrinking, all that reflexive desire to turn away—my body itself shouting "No, thank you!"—why did I submit to the contrary impulse?

The salient concept here is the well-known "fight-or-flight" response. Whenever an animal—a Komodo dragon, a Labrador retriever, whatever—is presented with a threat or perceived threat, it has one of two choices. Either it can confront the danger head on or it can bolt. No matter what it chooses, its body responds to the threat by preparing—quickly, very quickly—for action. The sympathetic nervous system, the part associated with the really primitive and reptilian stages of evolution, kicks into gear. Here is a description of this process, drawn randomly from a library book about anxiety:

> Activation of the SNS . . . leads to hyperarousal symptoms such
> as constriction of the peripheral vessels, increased strength
> of the skeletal muscles, increased heart rate and force of

contraction, dilation of the lungs to increase oxygen supply, dilation of the pupils for possible improved vision, cessation of digestive activity, increase in basal metabolism, and increased secretion of epinephrine and norepinephrine from the adrenal medulla.

You know those stories of mothers lifting cars to save their babies? Those are sympathetic nervous system stories.

The problem of anxiety isn't that the organism responds to threats by near-instantly powering up. That's clearly a good thing, species-survival-wise. It's that sometimes the organism starts seeing threats too readily. Same book as above: "Chronically anxious people exhibit a persistently elevated autonomic arousal level often in the absence of an anxiety-producing situation." Never mind the debate about how much of this is due to faulty wiring and how much to the organism's learning to *think* of harmless or not-very-dangerous things as potentially existence-threatening. The point is, anxiety is a neurological warning system, the sole purpose of which is to keep the organism safe and whole. Anxiety says one thing and one thing only. It says, "This right here? This right here is probably really bad for you. You should think seriously about taking off."

And taking off, or some version of it, is exactly what anxious people do. Sometimes taking off means staying put. The anxious person looks at his car parked in the driveway and envisions accordioned metal, melted tires, burning flesh—and he doesn't drive. He looks at a wedding invitation and envisions awkward conversations, drunken relatives, demands to join a conga line—and he sends his regrets. He looks at the gently undulating surf and he envisions jellyfish, riptides, stray hypodermic needles—and he sets up an umbrella and opens a magazine. At other times taking off means actually taking off: bailing on a date, ending a relationship, quitting a job, skipping town. But always it means the deeply felt impulse—the *involuntary* impulse—to escape. To avoid.

With Esther I felt this impulse and I ignored it. I was in the school choir. I had a glow-in-the-dark retainer. My favorite band was The Eagles. I had neither the mental equipment nor the wish to become the confidant of an impoverished married lesbian with a pregnancy fetish, particularly one I didn't much like. I didn't even need to articulate this to myself. My very being, my good old trusted, pre-cognitive, wisdom-of-the-body instincts, told me so—and I turned away. I plugged my ears and did the opposite.

I didn't fully understand this contrariness, or even much forgive myself for it, until I visited my mother in her office and she used a clinical term that none of my therapists had ever applied to me before, but that I immediately saw fit my brand of anxiety perfectly. The term was "counter-phobic," and it refers, just as it sounds, to those instances in which an anxious person moves toward rather than away from an object of distress. He moves toward whatever he is afraid of or made uncomfortable by because . . . well, there are any number of reasons. It could be straight-up masochism. It could be, it often is, because the thing feared by one part of the mind is valued and cherished, even worshipped, by another. How many great religious lives have been characterized by the fruitful cohabitation of trembling and ecstasy? How many artistic lives? How many performers experience terror in the wings, experience terror just thinking about waiting in the wings, but still walk on stage when the curtain rises? These are counter-phobic responses, and just in the world of music there are countless examples. Pablo Casals said, "Nerves and stage fright before playing have never left me throughout the whole of my career." The same is true of Arthur Rubinstein and Luciano

Pavarotti. Yet none ever stopped performing. The first time Tchaikovsky conducted an opera he was so panic-stricken and disoriented he held onto his chin the whole time—so, he said, his head wouldn't fall off. "Up to the age of forty-six, I regarded myself as hardly able to direct an orchestra," he later told a reporter. "I suffered from stage fright, and couldn't think of conducting without fear or trembling." Recently, Paul McCartney confessed that he used to get so frightened before playing with The Beatles that he almost quit the band in 1963, before *Help!*, before *Rubber Soul*, before *Sgt. Pepper's*, before *Abbey Road*. The Beatles without Paul. Think of it. It's almost as horrifying as a headless Tchaikovsky.

The counter-phobic impulse keeps people going who might otherwise crumble. More than that, it drives people to seek out what is terrifying. As a stance toward life it's a perversity, the higher mental functions flipping the bird to the lower mental functions. It's also something of a gift, both to the counter-phobic person and to the world. Because who gains anything from playing it safe? Who wants to listen to instinct if what instinct has to say is "hide"? Where's the fun in that? Courage, the writer Ambrose Redmoon said, "is not the absence of fear, but rather the judgment that something is more important than fear." The counter-phobic impulse is like that, and it's responsible for any number of things the world would be demonstrably poorer without: the Freedom Riders, the Velvet Revolution, Jackie Robinson, Doctors Without Borders, Lenny Bruce.

And yet it's worth pointing out that there are two pretty big flies in the heroic ointment. The first is that the impulse to disregard the anxiety signal is no more or less good by definition than the anxiety signal itself. In other words, just because it *can* be useful, productive, progressive, and noble to be counter-phobic doesn't mean it's *always* useful, productive, etc. Sometimes it's just stupid. For every Evel Knievel there are fifty morons willing to drive a motorcycle off a cliff. It's like the old saying about even the paranoid having enemies: Even the hopelessly neurotic have good reason to be anxious sometimes. The hard work, you discover over the years, is in learning to discern between correct and incorrect anxiety, between the anxiety that's trying to warn you about a real danger and the anxiety that's nothing more than a lying, sadistic, unrepentant bully in your head. The hard work is in learning to step back and analyze the data dispassionately.

In a sense, the counter-phobic stance would seem to be doing something like this. The counter-phobic person looks at his anxiety, judges it inhospitable to what he wants to achieve, and acts anyway. But in another sense, the counter-phobic stance is just that: a stance. It's an attitude, not as deeply embedded as anxiety but not fully conscious either. So it can be dangerous, because it muddies analytic waters that are already muddy to begin with. It adds another layer of difficulty to the anxiety problem. Anxious people have to learn to distinguish between their correct and incorrect anxiety impulses. Counter-phobic anxious people have to learn to distinguish between their correct and incorrect anxiety impulses *and* their correct and incorrect counter-phobic impulses. They have double the work.

The second problem is that a counter-phobic attitude doesn't mean an anti-phobic attitude. Just because you don't allow anxiety to dictate your behavior doesn't mean you're going to reap any benefit from your intransigence, clinically speaking. A moral benefit, maybe. A creative benefit. Possibly a career and/or ego boost. But will it be therapeutic? Not necessarily. Maybe not at all. Paul McCartney doesn't fret much before a concert anymore. But note again Casals's "stage fright . . . *never left me throughout the whole of my career.*" When he said this he was seventy-seven. He started performing at six. That's seventy-one years of unbroken anxiety.

Think about this for a minute. It's easy to applaud Casals's confession as a testament to his fortitude, professionalism, grace under pressure, love of audience, and any number of other artistic virtues. Probably we should applaud. But then stop and think what the confession meant for Casals the man. Think about the enormous, awful conflict it suggests. Casals's entire life was dedicated to playing the cello for the benefit of other people. Maybe the thing was pushed on him when he was a kid but after a certain point it became his choice; it became something he willed himself, that he decided, to do. Tens of thousands of practice hours, performances before queens and presidents and generals and aristocrats and more critics than you could count in a week. A fierce, monastic, lifelong dedication. And to what? To something that made his heart race like it was going to shoot blood out of his ears. To something that he dreaded so deep in the core of himself that not even seven decades of experience could ameliorate the sensation.

Think about how weird and self-destructive this is. Think about the mental contortions you'd have to go through, the thoughts you'd have to beat back, just to get up in the morning and keep doing what you're doing, to not be totally frozen by the inarguable fact of the matter, which is that you have chosen a life for yourself that makes you, a whole lot of the time, want to vomit. Think about how much you might not want to think about this fact at all, ever. Finally, think about how it doesn't really matter whether you are conscious of your counter-phobic attitude or not, that the very psychological perversity of your stance toward those things you dread is going to lead, either way, to more dread. Your temperamental refusal to submit to your anxiety is going to clash with your anxious temperament, and that clash is going to give off sparks. Because you haven't really done anything about the problem. You've just contradicted it. After my mother taught me the term "counter-phobic," I found an entry in the *Comprehensive Dictionary of Psychoanalysis*. There is, the entry reads, "a quality of desperation about the 'enjoyment' provided by counter-phobic actions. It is as if the individual is not really convinced of his mastery of his underlying anxiety."

"You're so mature! I keep having to remind myself you're only fifteen."

Esther was constantly saying things like this, and constantly confiding in me in a way that suggested she didn't remind herself often enough. She would waylay me as I shelved books and tell me her life story—or parts of it, at least, the parts that spoke of old traumas and her continuing quest to transcend them.

When she was younger than I was, she told me, her parents discovered her kissing another girl. Her parents were devout Mormons. They kicked her out and wouldn't let her come home until she renounced her blasphemous urges. Headstrong and self-possessed, Esther refused. For the remainder of high school she slept at friends' houses. She managed, through sheer willpower, to get good grades and to get into a good college. She paid for school by waiting tables and doing various odd jobs. And all the while she developed a powerful urge to have a child of her own, to redress the crime that had been done to her. Her husband had no illusions about her sexual desire for him. Saintly and selfless, he knew everything and he accepted everything. She had been pregnant twice already, and she had miscarried twice, experiences she spoke of mournfully. They were trying again. At night, they curled up under the covers and read classic children's literature to each other. "Then," she said, "we make love."

Another word on how alien all this was to me and how uneasy I felt hearing it—often while perched on a stepladder that rocked like a pendulum with the slightest shifting of my weight. For one thing, whenever Esther and I were together I had to keep a close watch on the rest of the staff so they wouldn't catch me giving comfort to the enemy. For another, at fifteen I'd never before met a professed homosexual. I'd never met a Mormon, either. At the same time, it was flattering to be entrusted with this information. It felt ennobling to be thought wise enough to understand such adult difficulties and preoccupations. "You're so mature!" observed Esther again and again, and I agreed. I wanted to agree. I still knew my anxiety as nothing more than the unnamed sum of my sensitivities. I felt so skinless at times! Things hit me so hard! It was a relief and an attraction to be informed that what felt for all the world like a handicap was actually a virtue. I wasn't weak or oversensitive; I was precocious. I didn't have a deficit of strength; I had a deficit of years.

It was dizzying to experience this revulsion and attraction simultaneously, and it was dizzying when, about six months into Esther's tenure, she came to tell me some important news and I whipsawed between the two. Esther found me at the back of the store, alphabetizing the Harlequins. She took my hand and pulled me behind the plastic accordion screen that separated the back room from the store proper. There was exhilaration in her eyes. "I'm pregnant," she said. She pulled me toward her and locked her arms around my back. I had to mumble my congratulations into the damp skin of her neck. I heard muffled words: "I just had to tell you. I couldn't wait. It's everything I wanted." The pregnancy was early. She didn't want anyone else to know yet. Anyway, no one else deserved to know. "I want this to be our little secret," she said. "Don't tell anyone."

There was something inordinately unsettling about this little conspiracy. Something about the present-tense reality of the data, about its physicality, both the sheer fact of it—a baby! a human baby!—and the way Esther imparted it, made me start scanning the store's perimeter for the fire exits. At the moment she held me, Esther's almost novelistic allure—her sudden, mysterious appearance, her outré sexuality, her exotic poverty—and all the flattery of her attention took on the spiky surface of unfortunate, unwanted reality. I'd never before felt so fifteen.

Then something extraordinary happened. A few weeks later I was back in the stacks, now on to the fantasy and sci-fi alphabetization, when Esther called the store looking for me. She was gasping and frantic. She said she was in the emergency room. I couldn't understand anything else. She begged me to come over. I pumped the pedals of my bike furiously. In the hospital, Esther was lying on a gurney in a tiled hallway, her face flushed and her stout body draped with a paper gown. She was calmer now. She told me what had happened. It was terrible. A cluster of cysts had formed in her uterus, little distended balloons of flesh surrounding her unsexed fetus like bubble wrap. Then they'd started to pop. *Pop pop pop pop pop.* The muted explosions going off inside her even as I held her clammy hand and mopped her clammy brow, making her double over and groan, pushing her baby out of her months before it was ready.

Where was her husband? I didn't know. I didn't care. What amazed me was where *I* was, which was a state of serene confidence.

It was the most remarkable thing. I still didn't like Esther all that much. I still felt uncomfortable with and about her. I was still my petty, brooding, easily disequilibriumed self. But in the heat of emergency that all was temporarily blocked from consciousness, sealed off from mind and body. In the heat of emergency I became something better than I'd ever known. I became doubtless. All apprehensions and anxieties evaporated in the fire of What Needed to Be Done.

I would experience this phenomenon many times in the years to follow. It would lead to a somewhat melodramatic sensibility as well as some wrenching confusions—a hunger for the dire and the tragic, and therefore a detachment from some important emotional realities. I was twenty, for example, when my father was diagnosed with metastatic colon cancer, and listening to the doctor deliver the news I felt, above a rivulet of doom and grief, a great cataract of excitement. Awful as it sounds—awful as it felt— I was grateful. A sick father was an excuse, a valid, inarguable excuse, to rise up from my mundane life, where anxieties teemed like mosquito larvae. It had urgency, his disease. It was like a magnetic field that slammed all other concerns to the periphery, creating a wide and clarifying corridor in the mind.

This kind of snapping-to of priorities is a familiar part of grave situations, of course. Something comes along to foreground mortality, be it cancer or a car crash, and we are expected to lay down our everyday concerns. We are expected to become less anxious, since anxieties are essentially big reactions to small, false, or inflated things, and death is so large, so true, and so solid that it demands all our attention or (here's the superstition, but who's prepared to sniff at it?) death will feel disrespected and attack. That's why it's so absurd—monstrous or comic, depending on how you look at it—when a guest at a funeral starts complaining about, say, her bunions. She's showing herself insensible to the triviality-stripping dignity of the situation.

This isn't what I'm talking about, though. I'm talking about something a lot less customary and a lot less useful, almost definitely a lot less healthy. I'm talking about an attitude toward emergencies that obliterates anxiety *and* awareness. When my father was diagnosed, and when he died, the rush of excitement I felt wasn't because the situation was going to be a portal out of the niggling everyday and into the ultimate. It was because it was going to be a portal out of the niggling everyday and into . . . nothing. It was a ticket to leave my worries behind for a while, that's all. A narcotic. Only unlike a narcotic, an emergency doesn't dull the senses; it sharpens them. It telescopes the vision so that you can concentrate on whatever the emergency demands, or on getting out of the way whatever tasks and obligations you have to get out of the way so that you can get back to the emergency. It's like Ritalin. It's like magic.

Sitting in a molded plastic chair in the emergency room of a Long Island hospital is where I first made this discovery. For four hours Esther cried and cringed and moaned her grief at her body having failed her yet again, and all the while I held her hand and nodded my sympathies, feeling calm and able—feeling, finally, as mature as she imagined I was. Sometime after nightfall I called my mother to pick me up. I had a quiz in the morning.

Within a month, Esther quit. I don't know where she went or what she did next. I don't even remember her saying good-bye. I only remember feeling, now that the emergency had passed, relieved—as relieved as all of the other nostalgia-minded, nationalistic denizens of the store—that things would finally be getting back to normal.

5.

the trip

When I was sixteen, my parents took me to a kosher deli a mile from our house to question me about my emotional state. Since my birthday I'd grown sluggish, withdrawn, and detached. I'd stopped making eye contact. I did even more morose skulking around the house than the average teenager. They thought something might be seriously wrong.

They had nothing psychiatric to worry about. The changes they had noticed in me were caused not by a dawning depression but by something greatly more prosaic: run-of-the-mill, dime-bag-buried-deep-within-the-sock-drawer, bored-teen drug use. I wasn't mentally ill. I was stoned.

To discover this, I'm sure, would have brought my parents little comfort. It was remarkable that they hadn't discovered it already. All the signs passed them by: the mounting obsession with The Grateful Dead; the purchase of black-light posters, pungent incense sticks, and a paperback copy of *The Doors of Perception*; the hair beginning to curl around my ears and down the nape of my neck; the insatiable appetite for salted pretzels and lavishly sugared cereals. They saw none of it. Consequently, when in the spring of my sixteenth year I asked permission to travel with my best friend, Justin, to see Phish perform in Binghamton, three hours north—Justin, with whom I'd recently raided our school's science supply closet, stealing a plastic graduated cylinder which, with the help of a drill, a narrow steel pipe, and a foul-smelling epoxy, we fashioned into a serviceable bong—they agreed without hesitation. I was a sensible, trustworthy boy.

It was a modest weekend trip, Friday to Sunday. Lodging was covered. We would stay in the dorm room of a mutual friend, Jesse, a freshman at the state college in Binghamton—a school that, since we were going to be graduating soon, we would need to check out anyway. The question was what we were going to do about transportation. For a teenager earning six dollars an hour at a part-time job, marijuana is an expensive habit. Greyhound and Amtrak were options, and Justin owned a car, but tickets or gas would make a painful dent in our party budget. And our party budget defined the trip.

Here is where Esther reemerged to cut the knot of our stoner dilemma. One brisk morning, without warning, she reappeared in the bookstore. Her manner had changed dramatically since she'd left. No more with the jaunty sincerity. No more with the gluey eagerness. And no more, especially, with the strenuous efforts at ingratiation. She was there, it was at once clear, to see me: to look at me, to ask after me, to thank me in some muffled, obscure way for all that I had done for her.

Cornering me behind the counter, Esther asked me what I'd been up to since she'd gone. What had I been up to? What is a sixteen-year-old up to? I went to school and I did my homework and I studied for the SAT and I smoked pot. I watched *Seinfeld*.

I watched Mets games. What was I up to? The only news I could think of was our upcoming trip, a little spot of excitement in the monotony of growing up well cared for.

"Really?" she said. "I'm headed up there, too! I went to school upstate. Did you know that? Did I already tell you that? That's amazing. Wow. What are the chances? When are you going?"

I told her.

"Holy shit! Me, too! I'm going to be driving up on Friday afternoon. Do you want a ride? It would be great to have company."

I called Justin and he agreed. I'd introduced Justin to pot, but he smoked a lot more of it, and invested more in the lifestyle. He had a bright-eyed, idealistic worship of the 1960s counterculture, particularly its communal parts. We were, in his view, simply accepting a favor the universe had brought us in its course, and saving a few bucks along the way. Now the cost of fuel and tolls could be split three ways instead of two.

Justin didn't know Esther. However cruelly expressed the clerks' opinions of Esther might have been, they had her thrift pegged perfectly. A week later, as she drove us in her battered blue hatchback off Long Island, through the thrumming tunnel, across Manhattan, and into weed-choked New Jersey—I in the passenger seat, Justin silent at Esther's back—she made clear to us, first by innuendo, then in the most explicit of terms, that the cost of our transport was the full subsidization of every aspect of the trip: gas, tolls, food, maps. She was carrying minors; we would carry the load.

I-95, I-280, I-80, I-380, I-81, NY-17 . . . it's all a blur of cigarette smoke and small talk, a case of retrograde amnesia. There is no bright impress of image until the hatchback rumbles across the Susquehanna River into Vestal and Esther inquires as to what our plans are for the evening. We have none. We will be doing whatever Jesse does, which, if college hasn't changed him much, is getting high and watching TV. The concert is Saturday night. It's Friday at dusk in the year 1994. Esther takes her thin eyes off the road, turns her small head.

"Want to go to a party?"

We pay for the booze, of course, waiting in the idling car—Jesse now alongside us, absorbed effortlessly into the evening's coming debauchery—as Esther trolls the liquor store, emerging at last with a bottle of vodka in a paper bag, a case of Molson Golden, and a six pack of Zima. Zima: the girl's guzzling beverage of the 1990s, a sweet fizzy thing like Sprite dosed with undetectable intoxicants. There is, when we are done helping Esther load up the car, suspiciously little change. Justin is rolling a joint on a Rand McNally road atlas, his work barely illuminated by the sickly light of the car's interior.

The party is on the second floor of a house that has been converted into apartments, on a quiet residential street a few miles from campus. When we enter it's discomfiting to find that we are by far the youngest people at the party, as well as, it would seem, the only heterosexuals. All of Esther's friends are gay men. At the time, this is a breed as exotic to the three of us as Maori tribesmen. A gay party! We had no idea. Jesse, with his easy smile and smooth cheeks, attracts fervent attention. One man, neatly dressed in a crisp white shirt, with spiked, inky hair, hangs on his arm for sport. "Just give me one night," he says. "One night. I swear I'll change you." Jesse declines but beams.

We drink. We do shots. We take long pulls from the bong on the table. We grow thinner and lighter and bolder in mind. Esther orbits around me, a blond satellite falling into a decidedly minor planet. Her seductions are unsubtle. But, then, she's working with pliable clay. To maintain a sense of safety, Jesse, Justin, and I spend most of the party together on the couch, and at some point Esther joins us and says, apropos of nothing, "I can come just by someone licking my neck." She invites me to try and, encouraged by the amused looks on the faces of my friends, I do. She is sitting to my right. I know this neck a little; we met under different circumstances. I know other necks, too. In the last few months I have had the opportunity to lick two separate female necks. Both tasted like vanilla. This neck is different. Esther's skin tastes like the sea on my tongue. And she is all business. Instantly she starts to moan. It sounds, my mouth nestled beneath her chin, like an animal at the bottom of a well. I lick some more and the tone creeps up the chromatic scale. It becomes staccato, reedy, sharp, a horse whinnying in the distance, agitated, diaphragmatic, clenched . . . until, with a sudden suctional break, she disengages, flushed and panting.

"See?" she says, smiling. "I told you. Isn't that a unique talent?"

The spiky-haired man reminds Esther of another talent she possesses. She disappears and returns with her blouse knotted at her spine, exposing a round belly pale as a fluke, with a deep, dark navel. She inserts a cassette into the stereo, straps cymbals to her thick fingers, and to a bassy oriental melody begins to dance. To me. To only me. A personal belly dance, as if it were my birthday at a Moroccan restaurant and my friends had sprung for the works. *Hum da-da hum da-da hum da-da hum da-da.* She lifts and lowers her hips on the axis of her navel. She makes the flesh of her belly roll rib to groin and groin to rib. She clinks and slithers toward me. Jesse, to my left, giggles. Justin, to my right, is too stoned to say a word. She is above me now, her thighs at my knees, undulating from the waist up, pressing her lips slyly together. The dance becomes less belly and more lap—a private transaction in a private room in a private club. Everyone is watching and smiling. You can feel them watching and smiling. Esther is smiling. She is enjoying herself, it's plain to see. She is enjoying the attention of her friends and she is enjoying lavishing attention on me. She is a depot for the room's attention. She takes it in and she metes it out.

Finally the music stops, Esther throws back her head, and the room applauds. "I took a belly dancing class in college," she says, as if this somehow explains the performance. As if, had she taken fencing instead, I might now be bleeding from multiple stab wounds.

Alcohol accelerates time; marijuana slows it down. Combine the two and time skips, hops, and twists. When in the night was it that, having gone to empty my bladder, I turned around in the coffin-sized bathroom to find that I was sharing it with Esther, who pressed her mouth to mine and ran her tongue along my teeth?

"Surprised?" she asked when she pulled away.

No. Well, no and yes. I wasn't surprised that she kissed me. The preliminaries had after all been pretty forceful. I was surprised, insofar as I retained the capacity for surprise in my state, by how inexorable it all felt. Your average sixteen-year-old heterosexual boy has the very lowest of erotic thresholds; a picture of Mother Teresa without her habit is enough to set off a minor testicular alarm. For Esther, however, I was unable to muster even the slightest sexual attraction, not even blitzed. Something in me, something stemming from the primary sexual senses—smell and taste, the hormonal faculties—balked. I didn't like the *odor* of it all. Yet I was shocked to find that none of this seemed to matter as far as what was going to happen was concerned. Not even physical disinterest could void the remainder of the script, redact and replace whatever ending had already been written for an evening that—and here was the crux of the problem—I found fascinatingly dramatic. Here I was. Here I was.

In the living room, the party was winding down. The music was mellower, softer. Exit music. Justin and Jesse were sunk into the couch with half-moon eyes, holding half-forgotten beers. I joined them. Esther, cross-armed in the kitchen, conferred with the friends that were left, nodded, crossed the room to where we sat, squeezed into the cushions between me and Jesse, and with frightful purpose said, "We're going to leave now. We're going to a bar. You can't come, obviously. But I'm going to come back. I'm going to pick up a girl and bring her here. Do you want to stay? I want you to stay."

"I'll stay," Jesse said.

She was solemn. "The offer is only for Daniel."

Daniel. It was a nice touch. She'd been staring at me the whole time she was speaking. The look on her face was sisterly, at once conspiratorial and oddly benign. I hadn't the foggiest idea of how I was supposed to answer. Were there questions that needed asking? Information to be gathered before issuing a response? Was there something I was missing?

"OK," I said.

"OK," she said. "We're going to go then. Stay right here."

And they all left. Esther and the gay men in the kitchen and, looking concerned, Jesse and Justin. On the way out someone turned off the lights.

I don't know how long I sat in the dark before the door opened and Esther entered with an olive-skinned beauty with a head of dark ringlets. She took one look at me, a strange, bleary-eyed boy, and let out a sharp laugh. Then she took off her coat, turned to Esther, and kissed her.

Ah, I thought.

Don't look at me. I'm ridiculous. I'm pathetic. I'm hopeless. I'm the late chapters of the Kama Sutra *illustrated in the style of* Archie's Pals 'n' Gals. *I should have watched more pornography. I should have done push-ups, chin-ups, sit-ups, leg presses, dead lifts. I should have drunk less. I should have drunk more. I should have masturbated less. I should have masturbated more.*

Don't look at me. Let me finish. Let me concentrate on my assignment. Let me try to read the cues, the limbs, the data. Let me figure out what this square sheet of rubber is for; let me stretch it just enough so that it does not rip. (Oops.) Let me lean on my hands, my elbows, my forearms, my forehead, your chest. (Can I lean on your chest?) Let me close my eyes. I think it will help if I close my eyes.

When are we done? I don't know when we are done. Are we done when I am done? Are we done when you are done? When she is done? When all of us are done? Do I have to make both of you done? When are you done? How do I know when you are done?

Now? We're done now? That's, well . . . all right. OK. Yes, thank you. That's nice. Thank you. I thought so, too. Ha! That's funny. Ha! Ha ha ha ha ha ha ha ha ha ha ha ha ha ha ha ha ha ha ha ha ha ha ha ha ha ha ha ha ha ha ha ha ha ha ha ha ha ha! Yes, thank you. I would love a piece of gum.

Hmm? Oh, yes, please do. That would be great. It feels late. What time is it? Really? Really? Wow. Oof. So . . . what should I do, then? Should I go outside? No, I think I know where I'm going. If they can get me back to campus I can find my way. I have money, yeah, I think I have enough. How much will it be? . . . Yeah, I have enough. Well. OK, then. OK. Yeah, Sunday. I'll see you Sunday. Right. OK. Right. See you then. Bye-bye.

[*Kiss.*]

The way I see it, the remainder of the trip is insignificant. Everything that followed over the next forty hours, all the emotional vacillations—the self-satisfied trip I took in the back of the taxi, my arms draped over the faux-leather seat in a tableau of conquest; the late-night shower in which I was suddenly overcome by the need to scrub myself raw with a fingernail brush and antibacterial soap; the compulsion the next morning to be tight-lipped, shielding what had happened from exposure; the compulsion the next night to brag, mythologizing what had been at best a blur of confused, mechanical heaving; the unpredictable fillips throughout of doubt, amazement, guilt, pride, disgust, anger, lust, self-hatred, self-love . . . none of it matters. None of it matters because in retrospect all of it lies buried beneath the avalanche of what followed. Even the car ride home, with its awkward imperative to make small talk and the breathtaking obliviousness of Esther's suggestion, made at a rest stop, that we send a postcard to the guys at the bookstore announcing that we'd fucked—even that, looking back, was just a car ride. Toll booths, gas pumps, coffee cups, FM radio. Just a ride.

No, it was only when Esther turned into my cul-de-sac and I pulled my canvas bag from the back of her car that the events of the weekend came sprinting and windmilling from behind to collide definitively with the present, creating the future. It was only then that the events materialized as my new, steadfast mental reality.

The house was quiet. My father was out grocery shopping.

Scott was away at college. David was at a friend's. I'd spent all my life in this house. How many hours beneath this one gray roof? Fifty thousand? A hundred? Once the roof had sprung a leak. Over months, the rainwater seeped into the attic insulation, the sodden fibers pressing down on the ceiling above the stairs, cracking it at the seam. Worrying the split one morning, Scott felt something give above him. He had to hold the ceiling up like Atlas until his arms went numb. Such was the force with which the mass fell at his feet that we were scraping pieces of insulation off the walls, laughing, for days.

In my parents' bedroom the TV murmured. My mother was sitting cross-legged on the comforter, folding laundry. I noticed my own white socks, my white shirts, my underwear. She smiled a maternal smile when she saw me in the doorway. "Welcome back," she said. "How was your weekend?"

That's all it took to make me collapse. It was a flood. Everything convulsed. Everything released. Everything upswelled. It was a sudden, nauseating pivot of the senses, as if someone had injected a poison into my blood that made even the comfortable sights in this reliable sanctum—the walnut jewelry box on the bureau, the carved whirls on the round tips of the bed frame, the last dregs of the day mixing with the lamplight—seem speckled and sharp with malevolence. Incredible panic ruled. I rushed to my mother, weeping. I told her everything. *Everything.* I told her about the trip, I told her about the party, I told her about the seduction, I told her about the sex. It was reflexive and without will yet still mortifying beyond experience. She cradled me like a baby, wept with me. She rocked me as I asked her, desperate, what had just happened.

"What happened?" she said. "What happened? You were raped! That's what happened!"

"No."

"I knew it. I knew I shouldn't have let you go. Those bitches! That awful bitch!"

"No. No."

"You were raped, Daniel. It isn't your fault. It isn't your fault. You're a victim. You were raped!"

"No."

"You were raped! You were statutory raped!"

6.

the dagger

It took some doing, but eventually I managed to extract myself from my mother's barbed embrace and shuffle off to bed. I felt that what I needed above all else was quiet. I needed space and solitude to understand the spasm that had occurred.

Bed, for me, was a loft my father had constructed out of plywood, two-by-fours, and a scrap of industrial carpeting. The loft's frame bisected the room's only window three-quarters of the way up from the sill, leaving a sort of thin rectangular porthole through which, while lying in bed, I could survey a narrow strip of our neighbor's yard.

This was our crazy neighbor. We all have one. She was raven-haired, ours, manic and unpredictable, a fearsome driver, a terrific shouter-at of relatives, and the owner of two breed-nonspecific dogs into which she appeared to have infused all her lunacy, like some immoral scientific experiment the ASPCA lobbies against. They never stopped running, those dogs. They ran back and forth across the yard, back and forth, from the driveway to the fence, yipping and yapping and whining and thinning out the grass as our neighbor, whose name was Dolores, shrieked at them to be still. This ad hoc dog run, the bane of the cul-de-sac, was my bedside view. It was what I watched, like a prison inmate, whenever there was nothing else to do, and it is what registered on my physical senses as I tried to calm myself, clear my mind, and think.

It was a hopeless effort. My mind refused to cooperate. Every time I thought I had hollowed it out the same mocking memory came rushing in to fill it back up. It was a memory I didn't even know I had, a piece of debris from a cable television sitcom I liked to watch. The show was about the adventures of an over-sexed Manhattan divorcé, and the memory was of a heartfelt monologue the protagonist delivers about the loss of his virginity. In the monologue, the protagonist tells how as a boy around my age he'd made love for the first time, to a cherub-faced girl in her father's basement. The experience had been everything a person could want from such an experience: sweet, sweetly terrifying, vivid, confusing, innocent. There had even been kittens involved. Kittens! A basket of them, crawling around and attacking his feet with their kitten-sharp claws as they (his feet) squirmed and undulated under the blanket. The experience had been wonder-ful. The excitement had been wonderful. The naïveté had been wonderful. The innocence had been wonderful. The whole point of the monologue was that there had henceforth in the protago-nist's life been nothing *more* wonderful. For all the sex he got— great sex, imaginative sex, sex involving sporting goods and fresh produce—nothing came close to matching the beauty and purity of that first awkward encounter and nothing ever would. He'd been expelled from the Garden and there was no going back.

But at least he'd been to the Garden! At least he'd seen what it looks like! The terrible message I took from that monologue, which played on a loop in my head as I watched Dolores's mutts sprint mindlessly back and forth over the same worn strip of ground, was that I had squandered that precious opportunity. A boy, after all, is only given so many cherishable firsts—they're valuable commodities, those firsts!—and I'd gotten drunk and thrown away the best one. I'd frittered away my birthright as a privileged American male. "Rape!" my vengeful mother had cried. "Rape!" And her invocation of that most innocence-murdering of crimes only increased my anxiety—not because I believed the crime of rape had been committed against me, but because I believed that, in a vital way, I had committed rape against myself. If rape is having sex with someone against that person's will then I was quite clearly a victim. But no one had violated my will but myself. No one had coerced me but me. I hadn't wanted to have sex with Esther or that nameless stranger. I'd had no desire. Yet I'd acted. I'd performed—and not badly, or so I was given to understand.

Why? Why had I done it? That was the stone that rankled as I lay in bed. I could almost feel the question lodged in the mattress, as if I were the princess and it were the pea. Guilt at least has a purpose; it tells us we've violated some ethical code. Ditto for remorse. Those feelings are educational; they manufacture wisdom. But regret—regret is useless.

Why! I wanted to climb backward into the past. I wanted to burrow back to Friday evening and decline Esther's offer, huddle drunkenly with my friends on the bus back to the college, safe and sleepy in the bright fluorescent light. Better yet, I wanted to go further back, to when Esther returned to the store, and decline her offer of a ride upstate. Or further, to when she descended on my town and my life, and adopt a more aloof demeanor, one that would ward her off, one that would truly be wise beyond my years. Or further, to the simpler days at the grocery store. Further, to elementary school, to terrors unformed and unreflected, to car trips, stuffed animals, Legos, Lincoln Logs, footie pajamas, picture books, to a time when adulthood meant the hushed rumble of voices floating from the kitchen up the stairs, down the hallway, and through the crack at the foot of my door. To a time when you could be drawn into your mother's arms, held, and actually feel comfort.

But no. No. If I had any doubts left that my days of feeling soothed were over, they evaporated when a soft knock sounded, the door creaked open, and my father entered my room. He wore a look of awkward concern, of some grim parental duty in the offing. He must have felt awful. It falls on fathers to prepare sons for erotic life, and his chance was as lost as I felt my innocence to be. There had been only one conversation, a few years earlier, and it had been too delicate, too obliquely executed, to make much of an impression. It occurred in his car. We'd gone to the store to pick up ingredients for dinner, and when we parked my father left the key in the ignition for a minute so that we could listen to the end of the song playing on the radio: "Paradise by the Dashboard Light."

> *You got to do what you can*
> *And let Mother Nature do the rest*
> *Ain't no doubt about it*
> *We were doubly blessed,*
> *'Cause we were barely seventeen*
> *And we were barely dressed.*

When the song was over he turned off the car, turned to me, and asked, "Do you know what that song is about?"

I honestly didn't. If I thought anything I thought it was about baseball, because of the famous rounding-the-bases commentary in the middle. As for all the heavy panting, I just figured you had to run pretty fast to get an inside-the-park home run. My father must have picked up on my confusion, because before I could answer he said, "It's about teen lust."

And that, in its totality, was the sex talk. After that we went looking for a sturdy shopping cart. And now here my father was, three years later, my big-hearted, soon-to-be-dead father, faultless, blameless, yet looking wretched.

"Mom told me what happened," he said.

Outside the dogs and Dolores were still at it, sprinting and shouting, shouting and sprinting.

"You know," he said, "I lost my virginity in less-than-desirable circumstances, too. I was in the army. Well, the reserves. We had leave from base for a couple of days and my friends convinced me to go to a prostitute. To a hooker . . . I lost my virginity to a hooker."

Despite the neighborhood's collective distaste, I'd always harbored a secret admiration for Dolores's dogs. Their total refusal to submit to discipline, to so much as acknowledge a command, had a perverse honor to it. On more than one occasion, leashed to a fence post, they'd simply chewed through their cords and resumed their sprinting. But now I found myself pitying their master. Poor, inept Dolores. She had all the tools and none of the talent. Against the energy of her beasts she could do little but scream herself mute.

"It wasn't great," my father said. "But it wasn't terrible. It just . . . well, it just was."

His head was level with mine. I stayed as still as possible.

"Pal? Dan? Is there anything I can do?"

After a while when I didn't answer my father walked out and closed the door behind him, leaving me alone with the dogs.

Of course I had to go to school. Technically I wasn't sick—not in a way the administration of John F. Kennedy High School could be made to understand without a rather humiliating high-level meeting. But I certainly felt sick. Throughout all the anxieties of my childhood, I'd never experienced anything remotely like this. It felt exactly like what I figured mental illness must feel like. And not just any mental illness. Not some romantic melancholy or discrete phobia. What it felt like was that I had been suddenly afflicted with a kind of diluted strain of paranoid psychosis, as if my head had been stripped bare so that everything—all stimuli, all perception, all information, all thought—was a grave danger, an assault on consciousness itself. In this powerful new state, in which memory and disgust banded together like some neurological death squad to hack apart serenity, there was, as in the most paralyzing cases of schizophrenia, nothing in the world that did not speak to my anguish. Everything was a malignant reference to what I wished had not happened and to the way I now felt. Everything was mockery. I couldn't even watch a commercial on television, because the mere sight of children playing on a swing set reminded me of the innocence I believed I had lost.

It was a state of total and isolating self-reference. I roamed the locker-lined hallways with a glassy sheen to my eyes—haunted, insomniac, shoulders hunched and chest caved in a perpetual cower, as if I were always ready for a car to backfire and send me dropping to the ground. I avoided conversation. I avoided friends, Justin in particular. I avoided physical contact. I avoided eye contact. I was totally focused on what was going on inside me.

And what was going on inside me? Remarkable invention! Creativity like I'd never known! A masochistic carnival! My brain was having a grand time whittling shivs with which to stick me, and it had no lack of material to fashion. Before then I had enjoyed school. All of the proximity—the daily crush of people, personalities, and outlooks—was a thrill. Now, to my horror, it became a grotesque pageant of lost opportunities, a parade ground for the display of hundreds of nubile, immaculate, fresh-faced girls to any one of whom I would now gladly have given my virginity, if they wanted it.

As distressing as the sight of girls, if not more so, was that upon my return my English class began to discuss *Macbeth*. It was the most excruciating assignment imaginable. The play seemed tailor-written to probe every one of my newly throbbing nerve endings. That *Macbeth*'s plot centered on serial homicide and not a premature ménage à trois was an inconvenience my anxiety had no trouble swatting away. My moist fingers pressing ghost prints into the cheap paperback, I looked down at the book and saw my reflection: a protagonist lousy with regret, desperate for calm, sleepless, self-torturing, self-isolating, self-warring, and so exquisitely tremulous that every slightest sound appalls him.

I read: "O, full of scorpions is my mind."

I read: "I am cabin'd, cribb'd, confin'd, bound in / To saucy doubts and fears."

I read: "Canst thou not minister to a mind diseas'd, / Pluck from the memory a rooted sorrow, / Raze out the written troubles of the brain, / And with some sweet oblivious antidote / Cleanse the stuff'd bosom of that perilous stuff / Which weighs upon the heart?"

And I read the doctor's response to this question: "Therein the patient / Must minister to himself." And the response horrified me, for it suggested what I immediately saw was an impossibility.

Minister to myself? How? This thing I was feeling wasn't something I could step outside of and examine. I couldn't lay therapeutic hands on it. I couldn't subject it to my will. I wasn't even sure I had a will anymore. My new state of mind had come on with such force and suddenness, such elemental speed, that it was as if the cord of agency had been snipped with a pair of scissors. *It,* whatever it was, was in control now, not me. How then could I minister to anything at all? How could you be your own doctor when you are nothing but patient? Maybe it would be better, like Lady Macbeth, just to find a nice place offstage and do yourself in.

Then, too, there was the dagger that appears before Macbeth, the fatal vision, clean first and then sluiced with blood, that he sees but can't touch. We read the famous soliloquy in class and I thought to myself, *It's real. The dagger is real.* I felt this with great conviction because as we read my own dagger of the mind was forming, not before my eyes but inside my chest. That blossoming of frost in my sternum—cold, sharp, ice-dry. My icicle. My twenty-fifth rib.

It is common to give superheroes extra-human senses. Spider Man feels a tingle when danger is imminent. The villain is throwing a boulder. The innocent has been launched from the skyscraper. Wavy lines appear above Spider Man's head. Tingle. Dodge. Thrust. Catch. Act. But what if the superhuman sense signals nothing but itself? What if the hero's only power is an inner alarm that rings to tell him he *has* an inner alarm?

That is anxiety. All that varies is the location and the quality of the alarm. Is it in the gut? Is it in the groin? Is it in the throat? The spine? The heart? The lungs? Is it a tightness? A looseness? An unraveling? A liquefication? Fluttering? Scratching? Scraping? Pulling? Is it hot or is it cold? Is it a presence or is it an absence? Is it a stone or is it a void? What do you call yours?

What do you call it? You call it what it feels like. Franz Kafka called his "the feeling of having in the middle of my body a ball of wool that quickly winds itself up, its innumerable threads pulling from the surface of my body to itself." Mine felt like an icicle and today, nearly twenty years later—sitting here alone at my desk, door closed, cut off from the world and all its threats—it still feels like an icicle. It is working away now as I write, dragging itself around my chest. It is still there, it is still real, and I still fear it. I still hate it, yet now with a nagging affection, the way a child feels toward a parent who has abandoned the family. The way you feel toward something that is both part of you and not, maddeningly. The way you feel toward something that has taught you an unfortunate truth, *the* unfortunate truth: You are not at the wheel.

How cautious is the anxious mind! It gives no quarter to error, it makes no allowance for reasonable risk. Being anxious is like being Dick Cheney after 9/11, trumpeting the doctrine of One Percent, in which a one in one hundred chance that the enemy has secured a nuclear bomb is transfigured—*poof!*—into absolute certainty. All further analysis nullified. Slice the numerator from the fraction. From here on out the denominator shall be king. . . .

I had AIDS. I had no doubt. I'd been infected with HIV. The virus, with its horrid Sputnik protuberances, was even now stamping out replicas in my cells, unwinding my DNA to read and copy the code, fogging up my life force. It was a petty fear, really—commonplace. If you live near a volcano you're going to fear lava. If you live in the rainforest you're going to fear malaria. But here's the thing: In your fears you'll be rational. You won't be crazy. As a matter of fact, you'll be hyper-rational. You'll be making excessive use of your sane faculties: the ability to reason and recognize threat, the capacity to apply logic. You will be nothing *but* intellect. This is the difference between psychosis and anxiety, perhaps the only difference. The psychotic fear nonexistent risks: alien abductions, microphones in the molars, demons in the trees, devils in the skies. The anxious fear actual risks: disease, dismemberment, assault, humiliation, loss, failure, success, madness, death. All the potholes on Future Road, all the risks distraction hides day to day from sturdier minds are, in the anxious mind, omnipresent and snarling. That is why therapists go to such lengths to urge their anxious patients away from intellectualization: The first step toward peace is disarmament.

I had AIDS. It was possible and so it was so. There had been a lot of mind-clouding substances going around in that living room. Who could say what had actually happened? How reliable was my memory of the event really? Maybe I popped in quickly without a sheath. Maybe there was a product defect, a pinhole, an internal rupture. Maybe transmission occurred during fellatio or cunnilingus. Maybe there was even a more notorious entry, now forgotten. All it would have taken was a momentary lapse and the opportunistic bugger would have darted right in and multiplied. Immediately afterward, I imagined, I might have been able to save myself. I could have rushed into the kitchen, snatched up a cleaver, lopped off the infected part. But now days had passed and it was too late. The virus would have made its way to my heart by now, and from there it would have been pumped everywhere, through every artery, every vein, every capillary.

The thought would not leave me. I was going to die. I was sixteen and I had $7,500 in bar mitzvah money in the bank and I was going to die. The unfairness of it was monstrous. It intensified my regret exponentially. Whereas before I had experienced the school's foot traffic as a parade of lost sexual opportunities,

I now began to experience it as a parade of lost opportunities, full stop. Everyone who passed by took on a distant, fading pallor, as if I were already drifting away. *There goes Laura, whom I've had a crush on for years. Laura with her freckles and her sweet wildflower scent. Laura, whose love I'll never even have the slim chance of earning now. . . . There goes Judy. Judy with her corn-silk hair and her paper-pale skin and her many gold bracelets. Judy, I'm lost to you now! . . . There goes Bradley, great friend of my early youth. Bright, talented, exuberant Bradley. Live two lives, Bradley, one for you and one for me! I won't be with you long!*

If this all sounds melodramatic, well that, too, isn't a bad metaphor for anxiety—as a kind of drama queen of the mind. If you have ever been friends with a drama queen you know how taxing it can be. To have one in your head is enough to make you comatose. This is essentially what happened. Another effect of my AIDS frenzy was a crushing fatigue. My teachers had known me as a voluble student, quick to participate and quick to argue. In response to questions, my arm always went up easily. Now I buried my nose in my desk and spoke only when spoken to. I shrunk from any and all involvement. In the early part of the day, when my anxiety still had an opponent in my sense of propriety, it was possible to hide this. But as the day progressed my exhaustion mounted. The guiding physical sensation shifted from the stab of my icicle to the weight of my eyelids.

To be fair to my anxiety (it is after all a relationship of a sort), it wasn't the only thing coaxing me toward unconsciousness. My mother was, too. Shortly after my return to school she began to mete out medication to calm my mind. Specifically, she sent me packing each morning with a small orange cylinder rattling with Xanax—then as now the most popular compound in the benzodiazepine class of psychopharmaceuticals and, with all due respect to friends and family, the contemporary anxiety sufferer's most reliable and cherished companion.

How grateful I was for those chalky little tablets! I adored everything about them. I loved to stare at each engraved name and dosage. I loved to trace my finger along the tiny canal scored down each midline. Washing a pill down with a mouthful of tepid water from the school's hallway fountain was like pulling a wool sweater over my brain. It cozied up reality, gauzed up the edge. Just five or ten minutes of waiting and I swear I could feel the chemical taking the reins from my frontal lobes, saying, "Whooooooa boy! Easy does it. There there." And then everything was better.

Is it necessary to defend my mother against those who would impugn the wisdom of packing sedatives in a child's knapsack? I hope not. It must have been terribly confusing for my mother to watch her youngest child change, seemingly overnight, into a patient. Downstairs in the converted den my mother sat all day with sufferers she treated but could not, beyond a certain point, love. Upstairs she sat all evening with a sufferer she loved but could not, beyond a certain point, treat. It was a dilemma of impulses— the clinical and the maternal—she would be caught in many times in the coming years, as she fielded panic-stricken phone call after panic-stricken phone call from her afflicted son, mentally flailing out there in the world. She didn't always navigate the dilemma wisely. For instance, it probably wasn't the best idea for her to have encouraged me, a little while after I became anxious, to make use of a relaxation tape she'd recorded for her clients. When you're three years old, it is lovely to close your eyes and bask in the sound of your mother's voice rocking you into complacency. When you're sixteen and struggling with a formative sexual experience, it's downright creepy.

The tablets of Xanax were a safer bet. Aside from the illegality of prescription-sharing, they posed no ethical problem. They were like soothing mommy surrogates I could carry around with me wherever I went. The only trouble was the fatigue. As my body metabolized the drug the agitation holding me conscious fell away, and I began to drool and fall asleep in class. This aroused suspicion. It also aroused an awareness that the pills were merely a stop-gap measure. If this condition of mine appeared to be what it was, not a passing episode but a mental sticking point, then I would need to learn to rely on my own strength of mind to get by. I would need, as my mother had before me—as probably generations of her bloodline had before her, dozens of wiry neurotics roaming worriedly through the shtetls of Eastern Europe—to become skilled in defense. I would need a therapist who hadn't breastfed me.

My mother found a therapist for me by asking around among her colleagues, and quickly settled on a kindly middle-aged social worker named Sandra.

Sandra. Immediately I didn't like this name. I had seen enough old movies to know full well that a psychotherapist was most effective when he (almost always he) was referred to by his surname and the word "Doctor," and when his surname was as Teutonic as possible. My strong preference was to be treated by someone named, say, Dr. Niedlehöffer, or Dr. Schlict, or, better yet, Dr. Niedlehöffer-Schlict. (An umlaut would have been very reassuring.) But somehow I doubted that there were any Niedlehöffer-Schlicts living and working in our part of the world. Friedmans, yes. Silverblatts. Goldsteins. Truckloads of Goldsteins. But no Niedlehöffer-Schlicts.

I would have settled for a Goldstein. The trouble with the name Sandra was that it sounded predatory. "Sandra" cried out to be said in a purring, smoke-cured voice. It was the name of some-one who sidles up to men in hotel bars.

Not that Sandra acted in a way that justified these associa-tions. Yet this, too, turned out to pose a psychic difficulty for me, for Esther hadn't acted in a predatory manner toward me either, at first—and Sandra, as luck would have it, bore a striking resemblance to Esther. They had the same thick frame, the same scrunched face and small brow, the same pale complexion. My demon, my confessor: It was as if Esther had returned to help me sift through the confusion she had wrought, only now she wore long floral skirts and accepted Blue Cross Blue Shield.

That is, she did when she showed up. My hang-ups weren't the only things getting in the way of a recovery. There was also the problem that my healer had some pretty serious time-management issues. When my mother was running late for a ses-sion she would call down for me or one of my brothers to unlock the door to the waiting room, so that her client could sit and read *National Geographic* while my mother changed her clothes or put on her face. When Sandra ran late she ran late off-site.

Her office was in her home, a stately wood-paneled house on a street lined with plane trees. At the appointed hour my father would drop me off at the curb and drive off to find a way to kill fifty minutes. I would walk along the side of the house to the of-fice entrance and half the time the door would be locked. Five or ten minutes later Sandra would drive up and rush out of the car apologizing. Once she failed to show completely. I sat on her front steps and waited. When my father pulled back up to the curb I was still sitting there—forgotten. This did not do wonders for the therapeutic process.

The question I still ask myself is whether anything would have done wonders for the therapeutic process. In sixteen years of anxiety I have had six therapists—as many shrinks as Henry VIII had wives—and five out of six have been almost completely ineffectual, like taking aspirin for leprosy. Without exception I have come to them in extremis and without exception I've left more or less the same—sometimes months later, sometimes years, in one unfortunate instance the same day.

I think I finally know why this is. It's because they were wrong. They were not, save one young man, incompetent. They were well-trained, well-credentialed, and well-meaning. They all had experience treating anxiety, and they were all familiar with multiple schools of thought on the subject. How they conceptualized their knowledge differed some from therapist to therapist; each had a slightly different take. Yet in practice each took essentially the same approach: They encouraged me to talk things out, pure and simple. They didn't get very much involved. They refused to be didactic, even when I pleaded with them. What they were up to was always slippery and vague. All seemed simply to be adherents to the old therapeutic cant: Let the neuroses unveil themselves. Release the steam through the valve. Let it out.

There is some wisdom in this, but it's a casual wisdom and unsuited to the job. Merely talking is calming. A receptive ear helps. But it doesn't change things.

A case in point: These days I am not in therapy (lousy insurance, not enough time), so whenever I am feeling anxious I pick up the phone and call my friend Kate, with whom I appear to share whatever genetic material that codes for hysteria. I called Kate just yesterday. I said, "Kate! Thank god you picked up the phone. I'm a wreck! I need to talk!"

"Oh, no!" Kate replied. "Me, too!"

"No!" I said. "What's going on with you?"

Kate said, "It's my health insurance forms. I can't do them! And no one will help me! I'm all alone here!" Kate and I also appear to share the genetic material that codes for an allergy to practical behaviors, such as opening one's mail or returning library books, but unlike me Kate doesn't have a spouse to pick up the slack, so she's devised an idiosyncratic ritual to get her through the shame of incompetence. Here is how she has described the process to me:

> First I walk around my apartment crying, with tears streaming down my face, and then, because it feels really weird to just walk back and forth crying, and also because I just can't bear standing up anymore, I get down onto the floor by bending my knees and then leaning forward, so that my face is on the ground and my arms beside me. After a while, this feels even more pathetic and ridiculous—in fact, I sometimes wonder if I get onto the floor to *prove* to myself how ridiculous I am being—and I get up, stop crying, and wash my face. And it's all over health insurance forms.

"So that's my problem," Kate said. "What's going on with you?"

"I've forgotten how to write!" I said. "Yesterday I said something dumb to a guy at the post office, something just totally not nice and dumb, and I've been obsessing over it ever since. And today I don't know how to write. I literally can't write a sentence! It's like I've had a stroke. Do you think I've had a stroke?"

"I don't think you've had a stroke."

"But how do you know? How can you be sure I haven't had a stroke?"

"What are the symptoms of a stroke?"

"I don't know. Look them up! Look them up online."

"OK. Hold on . . . OK. Here it is. Do you have trouble speaking?"

"I have trouble speaking intelligently."

"Do you have trouble seeing?"

"Umm . . . yes. But I think my contacts are just dried out."

"Do you have a headache?"

"Yes!"

"Did it come out of nowhere, like you'd been hit in the head with a frying pan?"

"No. I've had it since February."

And we go on like this for a while, until we're both feeling better. Then we get back to work.

And it helps. It feels good to be reminded that you aren't the single most anxious person on the Eastern seaboard. But it doesn't help for long. Talking to a friend who does not balk at your insanity is like having a stiff drink. It fills you with a glow. But when it wears off, everything is the same.

In my experience this is what most conventional therapy for anxiety is like, and it is what therapy with Sandra was like. Every week I would sit amidst the overstuffed throw pillows on her couch and respond to her prompts to unleash my thoughts and feelings as best I could. On the way home I'd be suffused with the same emotion I have whenever I drop a bag of old clothes off at Goodwill: self-congratulation. I'd made a step toward recovery. My body would feel, for the first time in six days, strong and unencumbered. Then, slowly but inevitably, the anxiety would swell again. A pinprick would stick in my chest and spread outward until the icicle was firmly lodged. My mind would shake off the least of its paltry training and I'd know, I'd just know: I was who I had become.

episode two

7.

freedom and its discontents

The pattern continued for six months. For six months I experienced a brief weekly relief and a quick weekly relapse. For six months—about four years to the teenage consciousness—all the activities that had once come naturally to me were as labor-intensive as if I were doing them in pudding. I couldn't study, I couldn't think, I couldn't socialize. Most troubling of all, I couldn't laugh. The most hilariously acid joke or outrageous pratfall rang hollow and pathetic. It was as if the world had lost some of the supports holding it upright and now sagged like a circus tent coming down.

Then, at the start of my senior year, something bizarre happened: I recovered. I was making no new effort, had no new pharmacological help, experienced nothing resembling an emotional synthesis or catharsis. I was barely participating in therapy anymore; for the most part I just sat there with my fingers laced, politely playing out the clock. Nothing outward had changed. Yet I started to feel better—and quickly, too. All I needed to do to reclaim my former self, it came to seem, was nothing at all. Time would do the work all on its own.

This isn't to say I became totally unaffected by what had happened. It remained naggingly clear that while everyone I knew was stepping up their efforts to remove each other's clothing I had stopped my efforts completely. But since a reversion to not getting laid was merely a reversion to normalcy, I wasn't much bothered. It still occurred to me that I might have contracted HIV, but as time passed and I didn't break out in sarcomas my paranoia deflated and I began, incrementally, to unclench. Each morning I woke in my loft less tremulous with the sense that during the night I had dreamed of catastrophe, disasters tumbling one after another like in some frenetic horror movie. The icicle in my chest thawed, then melted, then disappeared.

People with chronic anxiety may recognize this episode of peace restored as a false détente, a psychic ceasefire that in retrospect gives off the same aura of accumulating violence as the years between the World Wars. Because what everyone with chronic anxiety eventually realizes is that time, on its own, means exactly nothing. Time is just a distraction to anxiety. Its power to comfort is tied directly to its ability to maintain consistency. So long as the days are the same, so long as the ride is generally smooth, you've got a halfway decent chance of remaining steady. If you are a desert hermit or a cloistered nun, this approach may hold anxiety at bay for a lifetime. If you are a regular person with regular human relationships, if you exist in the flux of mundane reality, you're sleepwalking toward the edge of a cliff.

I can point with great precision to the moment I fell off that cliff. It was the day my parents dropped me off at college: Brandeis University, the only nonsectarian, Jewish-sponsored institution of higher learning in the country and therefore, presumably, one of the world's anxiety epicenters. I was standing curbside in the wet New England heat, my stout brick dorm—my new home—at my back, and I was watching my parents climb into their car and drive off. As they turned the bend and disappeared, all at once the frost re-formed on my sternum. My mind befogged, my vision began to shimmer, my limbs began to tingle, and I was suddenly seized by the impulse—an impulse it took every bit of self-respect I could muster to stop myself from acting on—to go bolting down the road after them, an idiot dog chasing a car.

It was bedlam. The campus was bedlam. Everywhere I turned hordes of eighteen-year-olds scurried around as if they'd just thrown off the chains of some vicious bondage. They wore expressions wide with opportunity, of almost limitless choice, of restrictions lifted, slates cleaned, surveillance minimal. They were joyful and unhindered, electric, confident. They strutted and flexed and postured heroically in the vegetal summer air. My parents thought they were dropping me off at a respected liberal arts college, but where they had really dropped me off was Jewish Mardi Gras.

I shuffled up and down the brick footpaths feeling like a health inspector at an orgy. Dodging errant Frisbees and threatened introductions, I considered every scrap of information on college I had picked up over the years, every campus movie and novel, every off-color anecdote from an older cousin or brother, every damaging revelation about the student life of a politician, and I found, to my chagrin, that I could not come up with a single one that did not proclaim, loudly, that college was a place where a person was supposed to let go. *Everyone* wanted me to let go. My parents wanted me to let go, my friends wanted me to let go, Sandra wanted me to let go. Mahatma Gandhi, had he been available

for questioning, would have wanted me to let go. More than anyone, the school's administrators wanted me to let go. Why else
would they have gone to such lengths to engineer this celebratory
atmosphere—all those orientation games and trust exercises and
mixers, all those quads primped and planted and manicured to
within an inch of their lives—if not to make me feel at home and
uninhibited? And why did I feel, in spite of their best efforts, as if
I had been shipped off to a gulag?

One answer is that I was supposed to feel this way—that it
was inevitable and even normal and I was just misreading the
signals. Over the years, my mother says, she has treated dozens
of college freshmen, many of whom experienced their first jolt
of true, consciousness-unmooring anxiety upon leaving home. It
seems that college-matriculated eighteen-year-olds are something
of a therapeutic cash cow. If my mother had told me this when
I was eighteen, which she didn't, I wouldn't have believed her.
The evidence of my pathological singularity was too prevalent and
convincing. But now the college's insistence on stuffing those first
days with activity strikes me as proof positive that not only was
I one of many trembling through all that manic, merciless gaiety,
but that I was, in a very important sense, in the psychological majority. All around me anxiety was rampant and I didn't have a clue.

For most American teens, college represents a first dose of
bona fide, adult-level choice. It means a sudden widening of possibility, a chance to think, love, and live in pretty much any way
that suits you at any moment, for pretty much any reason. The
freedom afforded by college happens to be exciting and desirable;
it gets the blood up. But what all those barbeques and mixers fail
to convey—what they are in fact actively designed to ward away
like a bad smell—is the converse truth that the freedom afforded
by college is inevitably also unsettling and confusing and deeply

anxiety-provoking. Freedom is anxiety's petri dish. If routine blunts anxiety, freedom incubates it. Freedom says, "Here are the lives you can choose, the different, conflicting, mutually exclusive lives." Freedom says, "Even if you don't want to make choices you have to, and you can never, ever be sure you have chosen correctly." Freedom says, "Even not to choose is to choose." Freedom says, "So long as you are aware of your freedom, you are going to experience the discomfort that freedom brings."

Freedom says, "You're on your own. Deal with it."

We're not as accustomed to thinking of anxiety in terms of freedom as we once were. The idea of choice as something that's prima facie unsettling to the human organism comes up often enough when we talk about the proliferation of lifestyle options— too many cable channels or brands of toothpaste or parenting techniques—but not nearly as much when we talk about the personal, private condition of anxiety. And yet for a very long time the idea that anxiety and freedom were linked was not only widely circulated but enormously influential.

The wellspring of this influence happens also to be the first book ever to treat the subject of anxiety head-on: Kierkegaard's 1844 treatise *The Concept of Anxiety.* Kierkegaard was writing out of a complaint that might have been directed at the organizers of freshmen orientation weeks. His age, he wrote, "was a cowardly age," in which "one does everything possible by way of diversions and . . . loud-voiced enterprises to keep lonely thoughts away, just as in the forests of America they keep away wild beasts by torches, by yells, by the sound of cymbals." To Kierkegaard, anxiety was a universal and ineradicably human experience, and directly linked to our spiritual selves. The subtitle of *The Concept of Anxiety* is "A Simple Psychologically Orienting Deliberation on the Dogmatic Issue of Hereditary Sin."

If you had to read that a few times to try and figure out what it means, try to read the book. Even Kierkegaard experts have trouble getting through it. Some scholars have argued that the whole thing is so confusing and opaque and generally out-of-whack that it must have been a hoax. I couldn't get through the thing myself; it made me nervous. And yet it's clear that Kierkegaard was writing out of intimate experience. His descriptions of anxiety are some of the most vivid we have:

> And no Grand Inquisitor has in readiness such terrible tortures as has anxiety, and no spy knows how to attack more artfully the man he suspects, choosing the instant when he is weakest, nor knows how to lay traps where he will be caught and ensnared, as anxiety knows how, and no sharp-witted judge knows how to interrogate, to examine the accused, as anxiety does, which never lets him escape, neither by diversion nor by noise, neither at work nor at play, neither by day nor by night.

This could only have been written by someone who understood anxiety from the inside. It's a sufferer's account. Even Kierkegaard's abstractions have the feel of lived truth. He saw that although anxiety is experienced as a kind of all-encompassing nausea—he compared it to the dizziness that afflicts a person when he peers down into an abyss—there is always something specific behind the feeling. That something specific is the popping up of an option—a crossroads. Before anxiety there is possibility. "Possibility means *I can*. In a logical system it is convenient enough to say that possibility passes over into actuality. In reality it is not so easy, and an intermediate determinant is necessary. This intermediate determinant is anxiety." Whenever a person is faced in life with a choice, his whole being trembles with the dilemma of what to do. It trembles because, being human, he wants both things but can't have both; because deciding always means being altered; and because alteration, however desirable, is always violent. Anxiety is the stage a person has to pass through on his way to creating himself.

You can probably see from this why *The Concept of Anxiety* has been called "the sourcebook of existential psychology." That we're all free to make ourselves and that freedom is uncomfortable is pretty much Existentialism 101. You can probably also see why Kierkegaard might appeal to a person whose anxiety began as the result of an unwise choice. But there's something about Kierkegaard's yoking of anxiety to freedom that's hard to accept, even offensive. This is a corollary to his thesis; it follows directly from the definition of anxiety as a sort of byway between possibility and actuality, a necessary anguish one endures in order to grow or develop or improve. Because if that's true then there are essentially two types of people, those who push through the anxiety and those who are beaten back by it. Everyone, in Kierkegaard's estimation, feels anxiety; it's part of the human condition. What separates the men from the boys is how you respond. Boys shut their eyes—they refuse to look into the abyss. The men look. They own up to ambiguity and conflict. They own up to reality. They are more tuned in to life as it actually is. A friend of mine who read a lot of Sartre used to say, "We all make decisions. Some of us more than others." Kierkegaard said, "The greater the anxiety the greater the man."

This is where Kierkegaard loses me. It's flattering to think that there might be some immutable suffering-greatness nexus, but it contradicts my experience of just how anxiety operates day to day. It contradicts a facet of anxiety that I find to be absolutely essential. I'll describe this by way of something I call the Roy Rogers Problem.

• • •

The Roy Rogers Problem refers to a meal I had seven years ago at the Roy Rogers franchise in the Grover Cleveland Service Area and park-and-ride, between exits 11 and 12 off the New Jersey Turnpike. I was on my way from Chicopee, Mass., to Trenton (long story) and had stopped to pee and buy washer fluid when, all of a sudden, I was struck by an urgent need for a roast beef sandwich. The problem—the philosophical crux of the matter— was what to put on the roast beef.

I'm talking here about your semi-liquid condiments. Some choices trigger one's anxiety sense and others do not. After select- ing and purchasing my foil-wrapped sandwich at the cafeteria- style counter, I headed to the fixin's bar, where I decided that what my sandwich required produce-wise was a single slice of whitish- pink tomato and absolutely no lettuce. I had no difficulty with this decision; I didn't even have to think about it. And yet the condi- ments caused me immediate trouble. I quickly ruled out mustard: I don't like mustard on roast beef. And the mayonnaise on offer was sallow and crusty, as if it had been left out for days. This left me gazing through the cloudy, fingerprint-smudged sneeze guard at the dark condiments: barbeque sauce and ketchup.

Barbeque or ketchup. It's a tough call under any circum- stances. Ketchup is the conservative choice—unassuming, sturdy, the tried-and-true way to offset the saltiness of the meat. In presidential terms, ketchup is Eisenhowerian. But what I began to wonder, standing there at the fixin's bar, was whether my life at that moment maybe called for something spicier, something as sweet and taste-bud-arousing as ketchup but with an edge. A sexy, bold condiment. A Kennedyesque condiment!

I deliberated for a long time. I scrutinized the tubs of sauce with their white nasal spouts as if I were consulting the oracle at Delphi. A dense knot of glassy-eyed commuters began to build behind me. Eerily, no one said a word. You would expect the patrons of a North Jersey rest stop not to have much tolerance for extended condiment deliberations. But that just shows how insidious our stereotypes can be. It was like they understood and respected the quandary in which I found myself. Like they'd been in the same position themselves. But there they were, breathing. I registered their presence. I felt a mounting pressure to act one way or the other. Barbeque or ketchup. Ketchup or barbeque. When you get down to it the difference is negligible. Both are genealogically related to the tomato. Both contain satisfyingly high levels of corn syrup. Even the difference in their appearance is subtle, the matter of a few shades. And so I got the idea—a flash of insight, really—that what I'd do was choose not to choose. I would apply a dollop of ketchup to one half of the sandwich and a dollop of barbeque sauce to the other and if they happened to mingle when I reapplied the top portion of my bun . . . so be it!

Then, just as I was about to execute my plan, someone to my right cleared his or her throat and abruptly, driven by a mechanism external to the deliberations I'd been making, I reached out and plunged a haphazard squiggle of ketchup onto my sandwich, then skittered away like a crab. That I'd done this, that I'd acted against my own rationally thought-out wishes, was, once I'd found a table and settled in front of my tray, a source of more dread and anguish than maybe I can convince you is true. But it is. In that inconsequential moment, sitting in front of a four-dollar lunch, I was almost as anxious as I've been at any other moment in my life.

And what nags me about this is that the source of my anxiety was exactly what Kierkegaard says the source of anxiety is, and what he praised in direct proportion to the volume any person possesses: possibility. The awareness that life is a series of choices any one of which could be either aggrandizing or disastrous. That this happens to be true I have no trouble signing on to. Anyone who has lived past the age of ten knows that even piddling actions can wind up having big consequences, and that even when you are super-conscious of your behaviors you can't know how things are going to turn out in the short- or the long-run. That's the drama of it all. On the one hand, your very existence means you can and will change things in your life and others. On the other hand, you aren't God, so everything is always going to be drenched in uncertainty and doubt.

The problem I have with all of this, the Roy Rogers Problem— or, if you prefer, the Vinaigrette–Bleu Cheese Dilemma, or the Häagen-Dazs–Ben & Jerry's Conundrum—is with the part that connects living-in-doubt to truth, and so to greatness. Because if you are one of those people who registers the drama of human agency every time he goes to the fixin's bar, then there is going to come a point at which an admirable receptivity to anxiety crosses over into self-involvement of the nastiest, most radical sort. There is going to come a point at which you are so alert to your freedom and the responsibilities thereof that you lose the ability to distinguish between those choices that are vital to human existence and those in which the likelihood that they will mean anything to anyone is so infinitesimal, so statistically remote, that even to consider the possibility is going to be a total waste of your time. And when that happens, when you reach that point, then whatever greatness you can lay claim to because of the atypical sensitivity of your consciousness will start to eat away at itself. Because greatness, with all due respect to Kierkegaard, isn't just a matter of having a sensitive consciousness. It's a matter of having a lot of consciousness so that you can turn that consciousness back on itself. It's a matter of using your consciousness to dull the parts that are distracting and harmful and build up the parts that are effectual and courageous.

Kierkegaard was right: To be human is to be anxious. But that's just the starting point. The next and most important step is learning how to discipline your anxiety without smothering it completely. Without, in fact, wanting to smother it.

There are two types of anxiety sufferers: stiflers and chaotics.

Stiflers are those who work on the principle that if they hold as still, silent, and clenched as possible they will be able to cut the anxiety off from its energy sources, the way you cinch off the valve on a radiator. It isn't hard to spot a stifler. They tend to look haunted and sleepless, like combat veterans, and they are more likely to chain smoke and pour themselves a drink within five minutes of getting home from work.

Chaotics, by contrast, work on no principle whatsoever. Although chaotics are sometimes stiflers when alone, around people, and especially in tense interpersonal situations, they are brought into a state of such high psychological pressure that all the valves pop open of their own accord, everything is released in a geyser of physicality and verbiage, and what you get is a kind of shimmery, barely stable equilibrium between internal and external states, like in those rudimentary cartoons where the outlines of the characters continuously squiggle and undulate. Sometimes the behavior of chaotics is interpreted by laymen as emotional honesty, but it's almost always involuntary. Chaotics are merely stiflers with weak grips.

When I went off to college, I wanted very much to be a stifler. Partly this was because of pride. To go crying to your mother right after you've had sex for the first time is sufficiently humiliating that it fosters a need to maintain composure at similar points in the future. Partly, however, it was because going off to college isn't just a journey into dread-inducing freedom. It is also a journey into a sudden, stultifying constriction of one's personal space—which is to say, the opposite of freedom. This is what makes college so precarious a transition for your less robust types. It's an anxiety double whammy: In the existential sense, college radically expands life's possibilities; but in the nitty-gritty, flesh-and-bone sense, college throws you into cramped living quarters with people you have never met and share no genetic affiliation with but whom you have no choice not only to endure but also to shower with, brush your teeth alongside, and defecate three feet away from. After close to two decades of cohabiting exclusively with parents and siblings, this shift can cause a fair amount of psychological friction. This is particularly true because in freshman dormitories it is something of an imperative to present yourself as poised and confident even if you are in fact bilious, angst-ridden, and actively decompensating. In this way, the dorms are not unlike army barracks, right down to the bunk beds, the thin mattresses, and the young men weeping quietly into their pillows.

It became clear very early on that, in these conditions, I didn't have what it takes to be a stifler. I tried. How I tried! In those first weeks away my circumoral muscles got a serious workout, what with me grinning anytime anyone so much as breathed in my direction. The grin was a reflex, like a startled cat extending its claws. I didn't realize how disturbing it must have come off to my new classmates until late one night I tried it out in the mirror. I looked like Charles Manson at a parole hearing. My other efforts presumably didn't come off much better. There was, for example, my voice. I did my best to pitch it somewhere short of screamingly hysterical but I could never pull it off. The problem was that the thicket of muscles that connect the head to the shoulders were, in my case, perpetually clenched—a condition that, had I weighed more than 120 pounds at the time, might have made me look like a villain on the pro wrestling circuit, playing to the crowd. Instead I looked and sounded like an enormously ugly girl at a Justin Bieber concert.

Then there was the coughing. I coughed a lot. It was a mid-level cough, volume-wise, halfway between a throat-clear and a deep-phlegm extraction, and I peppered my conversation with it liberally. I did this in order to quell the sensation that I was about to projectile weep onto whomever I was talking to. This sensation welled up in me especially when I had to talk to professors, and it was deeply unsettling, because I took it for granted that in calculating final grades a professor could only be swayed negatively by the fact that he'd been wept on. The coughing helped.

But not for long. By the end of my fourth week at school round-the-clock anxiety and the addled half-sleep that comes with it had eaten so thoroughly into my defenses that only the most violent fits were able to keep the tears at bay. There was simply nowhere to escape to. At home when I was anxious I could count on two places in which I was free to freak out as extravagantly as I wanted: my bedroom and the bathroom. Even in high school the bathroom was usually available for a quick nervous breakdown, because by then improved security had driven the smokers outside, across the property line. In the dormitory bathroom, I discovered, it was almost impossible to find the solitude a real anxiety attack demands.

Three times, out of a sort of neurotic muscle memory, I hurried down the hallway from my room to find a stall in which I could take my head in my hands and let loose with whatever high-order grunting or moaning might, when the paroxysm had run its course, result in an hour or two of calm. The first time I found a barrel-chested sophomore in lacrosse shorts vomiting energetically into (or mostly into) the middle of a long line of sinks. When he noticed me standing there (the cough) he stared at me briefly with wet deer eyes and said, by way of explanation, "Tequila." The second time the bathroom was being used for the same purpose, but now by a long-haired freshman who was naked save for a pair of tight turquoise underwear. The third time the sophomore was back, although this time he didn't notice me because he was unconscious. From the looks of it he had passed out in medias vomitus, slumped in a position that one would think it would be impossible to remain unconscious in no matter one's blood-alcohol level: his knees on the tile, his arms dangling at his side, and his chin resting on the lip of the sink. I took one look and hurried back to bed.

All of my weep-sorties to the bathroom happened in the morning, at anxiety's worst, and what the sight of my debauched hallmates suggested to me was not the simple, obvious fact that college students sometimes drink to excess and that drinking to excess isn't terribly good for the body. What it suggested, rather, was that drinking to excess was the comparatively smart way to go. We were similar, lacrosse-shorts and turquoise-underpants and I. We all felt the urge to expel the poisons within us. We had all rushed to the bathroom. What divided us was what preceded that urge. They had presumably felt pleasure before their collapses. Their nausea followed joy, and so had a sort of built-in redemption. My nausea followed nausea, and so was redeemed by nothing. I'd botched the equation. It was supposed to go PLEASURE→NAUSEA→DISCHARGE. Mine went NAUSEA→DISCHARGE→NAUSEA. What I saw when I looked at lacrosse-shorts and turquoise-underpants wasn't just a couple of puke-stained underclassmen but young men whose presence was explicitly intended to make it clear to me that my emotional life was untenable and self-destructive. They may have looked like schmucks, huddled there sickly, but the message they delivered was that I was the schmuck, for I didn't even know to have a little fun before the pain. And who doesn't know that?

My roommates delivered much the same indictment. Tom and Sanjay, of central Massachusetts and New Delhi, respectively, were not the sort to chase the pleasures of the flesh. In those first weeks, the majority were rushing into a haze of keg beer and bong hits and chopped-up Ritalin tablets. Not Tom and Sanjay. Would that they had, so that I could have been left alone with my anxiety rather than having to endure their unnerving equanimity hour after hour. They were geniuses of equanimity, those two. Tom, I could at least rationalize, had training in this respect. Tow-headed and rangy, he was a boarding-school veteran, and had the boarding-school veteran's nonchalance down pat. On move-in day he ambled into our room carrying an economy-sized bar of Toblerone, took a look around at the drab bureaus and the barren bunk beds and nodded dispassionately, as if he were thinking, "I've seen better, but it'll have to do." Me he regarded with a more quizzical air. He must have encountered that look in the eyes of classmates before—that first-day terror—but his attitude still suggested, in those first weeks, that it was his peculiar fate to have to live for nine months in close quarters with a Woody Allen protagonist.

Sanjay regarded me with the same wary skepticism. This really hurt, because of all people Sanjay should have been my comrade in dread and homesickness. Six thousand miles from home, unaccustomed to the strange ways of the American teenager, mandated at pain of disinheritance to achieve his way into a top medical school, Sanjay should have been paralyzed by anxiety.

We should have been up on our bunks trading pills like they were baseball cards. Instead Sanjay eyed me suspiciously, as if he were afraid I might walk across the room and collapse into his arms. Sanjay's presence exuded the worst message of all. To me his poise said, "I've got it way worse than you and I'm managing fine."

Or perhaps he didn't see a thing, for one night on his way back from brushing his teeth he stooped to pluck a small white something off the carpet. "What is this?" he asked no one in particular.

It was one of my Xanax tablets. My mother had sent me to school with a small supply. It must have fallen out of the container as I fumbled with the cap one dreadful night.

"I don't know," I said.

"It's a pill of some sort, I believe."

"Yes," I said. "It's a pill of some sort."

He paused to think for a second. "Is it your pill, Dan?"

"No," I said. "Not mine. I don't take pills."

He examined it, turning it over in his palm. "I wonder how it got here." Then: "Are you certain it isn't yours?"

"Let me take a look."

He handed it over, and I made a good show of scrutinizing the pill for signs of ownership.

"Oh," I said. "Oh, right. Yes, it is mine. I totally forgot. It's mine."

"But you said—"

"I completely forgot. It's mine. Thanks."

"What is it?"

"It's a . . . vitamin. It's one of my vitamins."

"A vitamin? What is it for?"

"My heart," I said, and climbed into bed.

8.

the diagnosis

It wasn't very long ago that homesickness was considered a legitimate psychological disorder. The French called it *maladie du pays*, the Spanish *el mal de corazón*, the Germans *Heimweh*. The English called it "the Swiss disease," because they thought the Swiss were sissies. Homesickness was a serious problem, particularly in the military; people died from it. In 1770, in his journal of Captain Cook's first voyage, Joseph Banks reported that the sailors "were now pretty far gone with the longing for home which the Physicians have gone so far as to esteem a disease under the name of Nostalgia." In a paper titled "History of a remarkable Case of Nostalgia affecting a native of Wales, and occurring in Britain," the doctor Robert Hamilton wrote,

> In the year 1781, while I lay in barracks at Tin mouth in the north of England, a recruit who had lately joined the regiment, . . . was returned in sick list, with a message from his captain, requesting I would take him into the hospital. He

had only been a few months a soldier; was young, handsome, and well-made for the service; but a melancholy hung over his countenance, and wanness preyed on his cheeks. He complained of a universal weakness, but no fixed pain; a noise in his ears, and giddiness of his head. . . . As there were little obvious symptoms of fever, I did not well know what to make of the case. . . . Some weeks passed with little alteration . . . excepting that he was evidently become more meager. He scarcely took any nourishment. . . . He was put on a course of strengthening medicines; wine was allowed him. All proved ineffectual. He had now been in the hospital three months, and was quite emaciated, and like one in the last stage of consumption. . . . On making my morning visit, and inquiring, as usual, of his rest at the nurse, she happened to mention the strong notions he had got in his head, she said, of home, and of his friends. What he was able to speak was constantly on this topic. This I had never heard of before. . . . He had talked in the same style, it seems, less or more, ever since he came into the hospital. I went immediately up to him, and introduced the subject; and from the alacrity with which he resumed it I found it a theme which much affected him. He asked me, with earnestness, if I would let him go home. I pointed out to him how unfit he was, from his weakness, to undertake such a journey till once he was better; but promised him, assuredly, without farther hesitation, that as soon as he was able he should have six weeks to go home. He revived at the very thought of it. . . . His appetite soon mended; and I saw, in less than a week, evident signs of recovery.

The Russians weren't so kind to their homesick as the English. When Russian soldiers were afflicted by widespread nostalgia on their way into Germany in 1733, the general in charge threatened that "the first to fall sick will be buried alive." During the American Civil War, the Grand Army of the Republic recorded 5,547 cases of nostalgia, seventy-four of which proved fatal. This was almost two hundred years after the diagnosis was coined, by a Swiss doctor named Johannes Hofer. The first case Hofer reported was that of a fragile young man who'd traveled sixty miles from home. The young man had gone off to college.

About a month into my college career I began to call my mother in hysterics from a pay phone bolted to the brick façade of the student center. By that time, the possibility that one could die of homesickness seemed very real. Being away at college felt like a kind of living death—an exile. The exile was of course from childhood, and it was permanent. There would hereafter be visits home, vacations, holidays. But if all went according to plan, this was it. This was adulthood, Month 1.

"I don't want to be here," I wailed. "I hate it. It's terrible. I can't go anywhere. I can't concentrate. I can't think straight. There's nowhere to go, there's nowhere to be alone. I don't know what to do."

It was the old anxiety incantation: *I I I I I I I.* The phone I called home from, every day, sometimes two or three times a day, was tucked into a niche in the façade, but not so well tucked that it was out of hearing shot of the students parading sunnily past on their way to check their e-mail or buy french fries. But that didn't matter anymore. By now the mental pressure had grown so intense that I was willing to risk exposure if it meant the chance of some relief. Specifically, I was after instruction. That's the second part of the anxiety incantation: *Tell me what to do! Tell me what to do! What should I do?*

My mother is one of those women, either unlucky or unwise, who lives by the maxim, "A mother is only as happy as her least happy child." But to her credit, she never revealed the slightest distress. For the first time in my life I became the beneficiary of the demeanor she reserves for her clients.

"Breathe," she said. She said it over and over again. It was her tireless mantra. "Breathe, Daniel. You have to breathe. If you breathe, if you breathe the way I will tell you how to breathe, you'll feel better. I promise you that."

The pledge was not unfamiliar. My mother is the Billy Graham of therapeutic breathing. Many years ago, she had little rectangular signs made with the word BREATHE printed on them in flowery epigraphical type, to display in her office. She owns dozens of sheets of neon-orange BREATHE stickers that she distributes to anyone in need. Growing up, one was posted on our refrigerator and another on the wall just beneath the kitchen telephone, at eye level. They were meant to remind my mother that whenever she felt unsteady, whenever the old anxiety feeling came back, she should sit down, close her eyes, and—

And what? What was this process by which the beast was to be neutralized? What alternate states of consciousness or bodily contortions did it require? I had never before asked, and when my mother had tried to tell me I hadn't listened. I listened now, and I was incredulous, for the change in breathing my mother preached was, when you got down to it, minuscule.

"Go," she said. "Find a quiet place to sit."

"But there *isn't* a place to sit."

"Of course there is. I've been there. It's a college campus. There are tons of places to sit."

"No, there aren't. The place is overrun. There are people everywhere. It's an infestation!"

"The library," she said. "Go to the library."

"But there are *loads* of people in the library! That's where they keep the computers."

"Then try another floor. Go to the basement."

I did as she said. In the periodicals room I found a wool-knit lounge chair with a heavy wooden frame and heaved it in front of a window overlooking a copse of trees at the base of a steep hill.

"The secret is to breathe much lower than you're breathing," my mother said. "When you're anxious you breathe too high in the chest. You want to breathe lower, in your belly. You want to be able to feel your belly rise and fall. When you sit, put your hand on your belly and feel it rise and fall as you breathe. Breathe slowly. First breathe in through your nose. Count to four as you breathe. Then breathe out as you count to six. Close your eyes. Breathe. Keep your hand on your belly. In through your nose, four, out through your mouth, six. In through your nose, four, out through your mouth, six. In through your nose, four, out through your mouth, six . . ."

I did as she said. I laid my right hand on my stomach, closed my eyes, and breathed. I felt my belly rise and fall. In through the nose, four, out through the mouth, six. In through the nose, four, out through the mouth, six . . . At first, nothing happened. It was difficult even to sit still, let alone to focus on the numbers. I almost stood and bolted for the stairs. Then, gradually, I felt it working. Somewhere within me things shifted. My blood chemistry recalibrated. Ions flipped their charge. Molecules realigned. The organism settled. Behind my eyelids the dark was now a dampening dark rather than the dark of terrifying space. I felt, as I opened my eyes to the bending trees, as I imagined I was meant to feel. I felt lucid.

My mother is far from the only therapist to tout the powers

of the breath. Anxious people breathe too quickly, and from the upper parts of the lungs, increasing the heart rate and throwing off pH balance and resulting in all sorts of unpleasant physiological changes. Learning to breathe slowly and more deeply is sound advice. "Once a client of mine can control his breathing patterns in a variety of situations, I believe he is 50 percent along on the road to success," writes one anxiety specialist. "For some people, identifying and mastering breathing patterns will completely end their symptoms and resolve their problems."

Unfortunately, this has not been the case for me. Breathing techniques have helped, but they haven't been able to resolve the problem—probably because my anxiety is so cerebral. For true change, I require higher-order instruction. Whatever help breathing did bring, meanwhile, it didn't bring for years, until I was ready to put in the time needed to change my habits. On that day in the library I was too desperate for a new mind, and too quick to despair. Sitting, all was well. I felt renewed. But when I stood up, I was aghast to find it all falling back into place: the fear, the tightness, the confusion, the icicle. And it was, for having been briefly better, even worse, like waking from a nightmare only to find that the waking was part of the nightmare.

Later that day, curled in my bunk bed, another image occurred to me—that of a series of strips from an old *Peanuts* compendium I owned in which Pig-Pen decides that it is at last time to go home and take a shower. There he is in the first frame, all fresh and combed and gleaming. Then he takes one step out of the house and wham! (he actually says, "Wham!"), he's back in his accustomed state of filth and dishevelment. What else was going to happen? Being filthy and disheveled was who Pig-Pen was, and he knew it. "I've learned not to expect too much from a shower," he tells Linus with admirable stoicism. "I have to be satisfied if it just settled the dust!"

When my breathing lessons didn't end my calls home—when they didn't even reduce their frequency—my parents decided it was time to pay a visit. On a cool Saturday morning they picked me up at the same spot in front of my dorm where they'd dropped me off, just weeks earlier, and together we drove into Boston for the most uncomfortable tour of a city since Mussolini was dragged through Milan on a meat hook.

My father parked the car in an underground garage and we walked. We started on Newbury Street, with its shoe boutiques and pearl-bedecked women window shopping; proceeded past McCloskey's orderly bronze ducklings in the Public Garden; past the sunbathers and loiterers on the Common; past the gleaming, gilded State House and brutalist City Hall; and finally made our way down the terraced slope of Government Center, where we sat to talk on a bench in the shade.

In hindsight, this was not the best place for my parents and me to stop. The shade in which we sat was cast not by trees or buildings but by the New England Holocaust Memorial, a monument which, I have always suspected, was engineered not to commemorate the greatest atrocity in human history but rather, in some perverse municipal joke or unconscionable psychological experiment, to evoke dread and fear in the minds of passersby. The memorial consists of a line of six glass towers, each of which is five stories tall and hollow. Into the interiors of the towers, which represent the six main Nazi death camps, the numbers of all six million victims of the Holocaust have been inscribed, and all day every day an ersatz smoke rises through steel grates at the towers' bases, as if to declare that even now and here, decades later and thousands of miles away, the fires of the Final Solution continue to burn.

It isn't just its design, however, gruesomely literal as that is, that makes the memorial so unsettling. It's also its location. For some bizarre, unfathomable reason, the authorities in charge decided to construct the memorial on a concrete island alongside one of the city's most congested downtown streets, just around the corner from the shopping mecca Faneuil Hall and directly opposite four—count them, four—Irish pubs. To be compelled in the middle of one's day to contemplate the mass immolation of one's European brethren is destabilizing. To be compelled to do so while a Paul Revere impersonator vomits in the bushes next to you is inhumane.

It is inhumane because it is liable to have appalling results. If you are already in an unsettled frame of mind, the sight and setting of the memorial could bring on a psychophysical onslaught of tremendous proportions—a sudden, almost revelatory flash of malignant-seeming power that overturns whatever mechanisms of biochemical equilibrium you possess, causing you to sweat, gasp, cower, tremble, and shrink, and that just as suddenly wipes out all of your cherished intellectual and interpretative functions, leaving you with nothing but a devolved, bargain-basement cognition capable only of the blunt detection of bodily danger, which it always, and almost always incorrectly, finds.

In short, you might have a panic attack.

People who are not pathologically anxious tend to think of panic as merely the purest form of anxiety. In the common view, a panic attack occurs when anxiety increases to the point at which it can no longer increase anymore: panic is the final marking on the anxiety thermometer. This view isn't wrong, exactly, but it is incomplete. Anxiety and panic are related, and the relationship is one of degree. But they are also, at the same time, radically different experiences.

To explain what I mean, here is an example from my own life. It's an unexceptional example, mundane and maybe boring. I'm truly sorry about this. I would defend myself by observing that anxiety and panic happen to be mundane phenomena, i.e., even when they are *caused* by extraordinary things like war and rape, they tend to *occur* when things are ordinary and predictable and relatively stable, against a backdrop of normal, everyday experience. This, of course, is one of the features of anxiety and panic that make them suck so bad.

The example I have is a work example: a writing example. It happened while I was working on the fourth paragraph of the preceding section, the one that starts, "It isn't just its design, however, gruesomely literal as that is, that makes the memorial so unsettling."

A disclaimer. Writers like to believe their job is tougher on the nerves than other jobs. They like to pass around cool, pithy statements to this effect, like this one, from the screenwriter Gene Fowler: "Writing is easy: All you do is sit staring at a blank sheet of paper until drops of blood form on your forehead." Or this suspiciously similar one, from the sportswriter Red Smith: "There's nothing to writing. All you do is sit down at a typewriter and open a vein." Or this one, from the poet Graycie Harmon: "Being an author is like being in charge of your own personal insane asylum." I don't subscribe to the exceptionalist school of writing, however. It's true that writing has psychological pitfalls—oppressive deadlines, poor pay, baring one's soul to an indifferent world—but so

do all jobs. Even the imperative to make choice after choice without clear guidance—allegedly the most nerve-wracking part of
the profession—isn't exclusive to writing. What is probably true is
that, for reasons having to do with solitude and a high allowance
for self-obsession, writing attracts a greater percentage of anxious
people than other professions. What is definitely true is that writers are better than most people at articulating their neuroses, and
more dedicated to the task.

So: the paragraph. I'd begun writing it the day before. My
goal was to finish it and then to write at least five hundred ad-
ditional words before the day ended. I had four-and-a-half hours,
nonnegotiable. During much of the period in which I have been
writing this book my workdays have been restricted to the hours
during which my daughter is at preschool—9 a.m. to 3 p.m.—
with forty-five minutes lopped off either end for travel, chores,
and sundry caffeinated-beverage-prep, e-communicative, and
excretory acts. Consequently, I have been obliged to use time
wisely, always aware of a very slim margin for professional error.

I got a good jump on the day. I was at my desk at 9:35 a.m.,
sipping Earl Grey out of an Aunt Sally's Original Creole Pralines
mug and staring at a legal pad on which were written the provi-
sional lines, "But it isn't just its design, gruesomely, horrifically
literal as it is, that makes the Holocaust Memorial so damned
unsettling. It is a matter, also, of its terrible location." This was
encouraging. They were awful lines, but it was easy to see why
they were awful. By 9:50, after some preliminary dawdling, I'd
managed to amputate the most offensive bits, editing the lines
down to, "But it isn't just its design, gruesomely literal as it is,
that makes the memorial so damned unsettling. It is a matter,
also, of its terrible location." By 9:55 I'd changed "it" to "that" in
the first sentence and cut "terrible" from the second sentence. At

9:57 I cut the starting conjunction and squeezed an "however" in there. At 9:59 I cut "damned." At 10:02 I contracted "it is," cut "a matter" and "of," and took "also" out of commas. It was a nice run. After twenty-seven minutes, I was ready to move forward into actual writing.

The blank space in front of me didn't feel like a Fowlerian void. I knew what came next. I had strong memories of the incongruence between the memorial and its setting. I remembered the pubs and the smell of stale Guinness that wafted out when someone opened a door. I remembered Faneuil Hall being nearby because I could never forget the image of tourists eating clam chowder with sporks as they read the famous Niemöller poem off a plaque at the memorial's base, the poem that starts, "First they came for the Communists, and I didn't speak up because I wasn't a Communist." I had indeed once seen a Colonial impersonator puke beside the memorial, and for some reason I was pretty sure he was supposed to be Paul Revere. But what occurred to me as I stared at the page was that my memories weren't detailed enough. This all happened fifteen years ago. How many pubs were there? Where exactly was Faneuil Hall vis-à-vis the memorial? Are there in fact bushes beside the monument into which Paul Revere could vomit?

To answer these questions, I turned to the Internet. What did memoirists do before Google Maps? I dragged the cute yellow homunculus onto Congress Street and clicked on those floating white carets that glide you digitally down the road. I clicked the "Satellite" button and surveyed Boston like God, or a Kennedy. I typed "bar" into the "Search nearby" field and counted all the red balloons that popped up. I was having a good time. And that was when, drifting comfortably in cyberspace, I began to sense my mind slipping off its moorings. It was a cognitive slipping.

My thoughts began to drift from the screen and alight on other things, peripheral things: what I was going to make for dinner that night; what my daughter had meant when on the way to school that morning she'd said, "poopy is fun!" (how was poopy fun, exactly? making it? flushing it? *playing* with it? I should find out); whether I should commence defensive tactics against the hairs that had already taken over my shoulders and upper back and were now threatening to march south; whether it was going to rain; why, despite more than three decades of life, I still hadn't been to Montana . . .

All this was typical, of course. Everyone gets distracted. What wasn't typical was what followed, which was the emergence and blossoming of anxiety. It started with a simple effort to regain focus. At first I was able to swat away most of the distracting thoughts, like gnats. But like gnats, the thoughts always returned, and in force, so that before long swatting them away changed from an effort to get back to my primary occupation to the primary occupation itself. *I* changed, sitting there at my computer, from a writer to a thought-swatter.

That was Phase One: the thought swarm. Phase Two was a perplexity about what to do next, a desire to find a way back to a state of undistracted productivity. This phase didn't last long. It never does, because the thing about thought swarms is that not only do they make rational, directed thinking hard to come by, they make the *effort* at rational thinking so frustrating that all you want to do is escape. And so I soon entered Phase Three. This was the self-hatred phase, in which my energy went toward demeaning myself for being the sort of writer who allows himself to become distracted and confused after only an hour of work, which is to say the bad kind, the kind doomed to failure. At this point I made the mistake of looking at the clock. It was half-past noon, which meant that my workday was halfway done, which meant that my workday was halfway wasted, wasted by my ineptitude and lack of psychic strength, an analysis that conjured an image of my editor, a really lovely woman who likes me and wants to see me succeed, deleting my name from her electronic Rolodex, shaking her head as she does because she can't believe she was foolish enough to sign up a writer whose potential was so obviously fated to be destroyed by his weaknesses—the very weaknesses that were supposed to be the subject of the book she had signed up, which made it all that much sadder. And that—at around 12:40—is when I began to hyperventilate, sweat, and look nervously around me, and make little birdlike chirping noises, and run my fingers through my prematurely graying hair like those put-upon middle-aged men in commercials for tax-prep services. That's when I began to tremble, and cry a little. That's when the desire mounted to go running out of my office, out into the street, and down the block, in order to burn off the overwhelming sense that I had doomed myself because of a couple of hours of tough writing. That's when, instead of running down the block, I called Kate and, getting her voicemail, laid my head on my desk, closed my eyes, and begged whoever might be listening for a half-hour of blissful unconsciousness. Just a half-hour, to reset my nervous system.

This was an unpleasant experience, and pretty much ruined the rest of the day. But it wasn't a panic attack. It was what I would call an anxiety attack—an 8.3, I would calculate, on my personal anxiety scale. The scale runs from zero to ten, zero being catatonic and ten being the guy in Edvard Munch's *The Scream*, where, psychologically speaking, you're on a bridge surrounded by faceless strangers who are unable or unwilling to help you and the sky is blood-orange red and swirling and hectic and everything is so bleak and awful that you'd rather die than spend another second where you are.

A panic attack is worse than that. A panic attack is off the charts. A panic attack means you've ascended through every stage on the scale and then broken right off it, fallen right off the edge of the earth into some kind of neurotic *satori*, where anxiety isn't even a factor anymore because anxiety is related to thinking, and with panic there is no thinking. Panic is pure reflex. It is a reversion to a state of being in which you are a kind of puppet to forces above and outside you, forces whose only purpose, once they have caused you to panic, is to get you to stop panicking. When you are in the midst of a panic attack you are no longer human. You are no longer a reasoning being. You are an animal under attack, indistinguishable from the animals whose panic Charles Darwin, who himself suffered from crippling panic attacks, described in *The Expression of the Emotions in Man and Animals*:

> With all or almost all animals, even with birds, terror causes the body to tremble. The skin becomes pale, sweat breaks out, and the hair bristles. The secretions of the alimentary canal and of the kidneys are increased, and they are involuntarily voided, owing to the relaxation of the sphincter muscles, as is known to be the case with man, and as I have seen with cattle, dogs, cats, and monkeys. The breathing is hurried. The heart beats quickly, wildly, and violently; but whether it pumps the blood more efficiently through the body may be doubted, for the surface seems bloodless and the strength of the muscles soon fails. In a frightened horse I have felt through the saddle the beating of the heart so plainly that I could have counted the beats. The mental faculties are much disturbed. Utter prostration soon

follows, and even fainting. A terrified canary-bird has been seen not only to tremble and to turn white about the base of the bill, but to faint; and I once caught a robin in a room, which fainted so completely, that for a time I thought it dead.

All through our walk across Boston my anxiety hovered at around a 5.5 on my anxiety scale. The comfort of my parents' presence might have tamped it below the halfway mark (no small accomplishment) had I not been mortified that they'd had to come all this way, or if their coming wasn't going to be followed in less than thirty-six hours by their leaving, either with me, which would be unspeakably shameful, or without me, which would be unspeakably awful. The point at which the mental needle started to migrate upward was, first, when the Holocaust Memorial came into view, shouting *Genocide! Genocide!,* and then again when my parents and I found a bench and my father started to talk. We were seated in front of a bronze statue of a man from a different era, wearing that era's uncomfortable clothes. Beyond that were the towers and the fake smoke and the tourists strolling through it all, and, farther still, the strenuously charming trattorias of the North End, where we'd decided to go for lunch. I thought I caught my father looking pleadingly in their direction before he draped his arm over my shoulder and said, "So. Pal. How are you doing?"

I cleared my throat.

"We've been pretty worried about you," he said. "All those calls. We know it's been tough."

It's remarkable just how quickly mental weather can go extreme. We were only twenty words and one participant into the conversation and already I could feel the hysteria rising up in me like coffee in a percolator. I felt I couldn't allow it to spill over.

Not in front of my father, whom I wanted to see in me at least the semblance of masculine fortitude, and not in front of my mother—not again. Not now that I had packed up and said my good-byes. Not now that I had reached the age of legal maturity and therefore, I felt (being far stupider than I realized), of mental self-sufficiency. There seemed to be large matters of propriety and self-respect at stake, and so I lowered my head and focused my eyes on the small patch of scuffed brick at my feet; just a glance at the memorial or my parents' worried faces, or even at the faces of normal human pedestrians, and I knew I'd be a goner. And I clenched—a Herculean, full-body-and-mind clenching. Never in my life have I concentrated so intently on making sure that every muscle, organ, membrane, and thought are held in static check. The only common analogy I can think of is the state of being at once exceedingly nauseated and dead-set on not vomiting. I found a quivering equilibrium.

Then my mother took over.

"I know how you're feeling," she said. "I've been where you are. I see it in my patients every day. You're confused and you're scared." I braced myself. The bricks at my feet seemed to soften. "I can see the anxiety in your eyes. You're staring at everything like it's going to jump out and grab you around the neck. I know what it feels like to be vigilant like that. It's horrible. It's awful. You feel like you're going crazy." I heard a spate of giggles in the distance, from just around the spot where the crowd emerges from faux-Buchenwald into the open air. Things began to loosen further. "You feel like something terrible is going to happen at any moment. It's awful. *Awful.*" Something, curiosity or fear, compelled me to glance up and I saw a group of teenage girls walking away from the monument licking lollipops. *Lollipops!* I quickly put my head back down. "But nothing bad is going to happen to you, Daniel. I promise you. Nothing bad is going to happen. You're not dying. You're not going crazy. It just *feels* like you're going crazy. But that's all this is. You have to see that. That's all it is: a feeling. It isn't real. It's just a feeling."

There was a slim part of me, an intellectual sliver located somewhere in my prefrontal cortex, that wanted to argue with my mother regarding the distinction between feelings and reality. Was there one? Really? It didn't seem like it. But that part was quickly subsumed by the rising anxiety, which now reached the point at which tears were unavoidable. My mother saw them begin to fall.

"Oh, Daniel," she said, stroking my back between my shoulder blades. "You're not crazy. Honey, you're going to be okay. You're just anxious. You have severe anxiety . . . like me. It's a mental disorder, that's all. You just need some help to get you through it. Therapy. Some medication. You have a condition, a treatable condition."

And with that—my first ever diagnosis—my anxiety at last breached the borders. *Like me.* On a concrete island two hundred miles from home I'd unwittingly attended my own coronation, and I saw at once that there was little hope of abdication. Darwin was right about panic: the hairs bristle, the breathing is hurried, the muscles fail, the mental faculties are much disturbed. Utter prostration soon followed.

9.

an actor prepares

My parents said I could come home with them if I wanted. It was the easiest thing there was. I would just need to pack my things and we'd head for the interstate. We could call the registrar's office from the road. But I decided to stick it out, and from the way my parents nodded their heads I could tell they were pleased. What purpose would I serve at home? What good would it do me to putter aimlessly around the house? I would sleep for twelve hours a day and read for a few more. What would I do with the remaining nine?

But there was a catch. If I was going to stay at school, my mother insisted, I would have to seek professional help. "There are two-and-a-half months between now and winter break," she said. "There's no reason you should have to get through that time on your own. A trained therapist, someone to talk to and learn from, could be an enormous help. It's the only way, sweetheart."

And that is how, on the Tuesday after my panic attack, I found myself frozen in a paranoiac haze on the border between the road that encircled the campus and the asphalt footpath that led to the university's behavioral-health center.

It was early in the morning. There was no one on the road behind me and no one on the path in front of me. All the blinds in the windows of the building that housed the center were shut against the morning sun. I was alone. Yet I felt as if I were about to waltz onto the stage at Carnegie Hall. Standing there with just a short distance to cover—a mere eighty feet lay between me and the center's front door—I was thoroughly convinced that once I started walking a multitude of eyes from every direction would lock onto me, all of them hungry for the sight of a student actually freaked out enough to visit the campus shrink, like those eighteenth-century Londoners who'd head to the madhouse on an idle Sunday to ogle psychotics.

I was determined to avoid such a humiliation. There had been too many humiliations, too many compromises, already. The trouble was, my determination left me with only two options as to how to proceed. I could abort mission, continuing along the road until it looped back to my dorm, after which I would be duty-bound to return home; or I could labor against every impulse in my being to affect a demeanor contrary to my actual state, so that anyone who saw me make the trip from curb to clinic would be unable to imagine that I was doing so for therapy. In short, I could give up or I could try to fake it.

I decided on the second.

When I was eight years old, I auditioned for and won a part in a regional traveling production of the musical *Oliver!* I was one of Fagin's kids, a coal-smudged thief in an oversized tweed cap. It wasn't a speaking part, but it did include a featured moment. In

Act I, right after singing an ode to the pleasures of pickpocketing, the boys have a laugh at Fagin's expense. Fagin enters the room, the boys get scared, and they hush up one by one until there is a single, oblivious laugher remaining: me.

I prepared for that moment as if I were DeNiro preparing for *Raging Bull*. I studied the actors in my favorite TV shows to see how they laughed. I practiced each evening in the bathroom mirror, thinking comic thoughts, running the faucet at full volume so my brothers wouldn't hear me. I tracked down every reference to orphans in the *Encyclopædia Britannica*, hoping to find clues as to how one would experience mirth. But no matter how hard I worked I could not get that laugh to sound natural. At one of our last performances, at an outdoor festival, my father discovered me behind the costume trailer only minutes before curtain, still testing out variations.

"Ha ha ha! Hee hee hee! Ho ho ho! Mwah ha ha! Heh heh heh! Tee hee hee! Hrump hrump hrump!"

"Just laugh like yourself," my father said.

When the run ended, I quit the theater forever.

I mention this failure because the theatrical task I faced a decade later was exponentially more difficult than having to produce an authentic laugh. To make myself appear casual and unperturbed while in the throes of paranoia and terror seemed not only challenging but impossible.

The first obstacle, as I see it now, was physical. Professional actors are forever having to contend with the limitations of their bodies. Wallace Shawn, for example, is a gifted and experienced actor, but slight, gnomish, and reedy-voiced as he is he'll never play a thug or soldier except for comic effect. Some things you just can't change. For the anxiety sufferer trying to come off as normal, the limitations of the body are complicated by the fact that the body he has is no longer the one he's always known. His body has *already* changed, and what he inhabits is alien and uncomfortable. He isn't trying to transform himself into something different; he's trying to transform someone different back into himself.

On that October morning, paralyzed there on the cusp of therapy, anxiety had transformed my appearance as thoroughly as if I'd swallowed Jekyll's potion. My back was knotted and hunched, my shoulders were up to my ears, my skin was pallid and clammy, my cheeks were gaunt, and my fingertips were torn and scabbed from my gnawing at them day and night. Years later, in a biography of William James, I would come across a self-portrait he'd drawn during his own youthful bout with depression and anxiety:

I looked like a standing version of this. I would've preferred to have looked like this:

There is a good psychological reason why it is so difficult to change how you look once you are deep into anxiety. Before getting into that reason, however, it's worth pausing to say more about those gnawed fingers, for the habit that got them into such bad shape is both one of the most familiar and most misunderstood aspects of anxiety. Nail-biting—that tell-tale sign of addled nerves—is more than just an unattractive tendency or cosmetic violation, as is commonly thought. It's a scourge.

An example: Right now, as I write, I am looking at the ring finger of my left hand. I write, when I am writing by hand, with my right hand, which means that when I am anxious I am free to chew on the nails of my left hand as I work. This doesn't help the process of composition—it doesn't improve thought—but it gives the *illusion* of helping composition, which is enough and maybe even the same thing, in the end. I have been chewing on this particular nail for three days, bit by tiny bit, snipping off just enough with each mouth-entry to satisfy my compulsion but not so much that I'll put myself out of business altogether.

This morning, though, there was an accident. I got a satisfying tag of nail between my teeth and, distracted by an uncooperative sentence, I put too much oomph into the follow-through and tore off a strip of nail about a sixteenth of an inch in width. This exposed the soft, spongy flesh beneath, which ballooned out like the ice cream in an ice cream sandwich when it's had too much time to melt and you hold it too tightly.

How to describe the pain that results when the nail bed comes into contact with air? What it feels like, until the nail grows back over the exposed area, is like a fusillade of microscopic knitting needles being fired by a battery of tiny howitzers poised at around the level of the first knuckle. And this pain, as the result of some neuroelectrical mechanism or other, reverberates inwardly even as it is being shot outwardly: The joints start to ache. There's an inflammatory aspect to the experience. Then the heart gets involved. Informed of the insult, it sends some extra blood to the region, to facilitate healing. But it feels like what the heart has sent is *itself*, like it has assessed the situation and decided that the best thing for it to do is to pull up stakes and bivouac right there in the fingertip until things blow over. Which means a new, heightened, rhythmic type of pain, a *Looney Tunes* pulsation that unlike in cartoons doesn't go away quickly because there the nail bed is, newbornishly exposed, which it will remain for a long time because human nails grow surprisingly slowly.

I've experienced some pain in my time: fractured digits, lacerations, dislocations, sprains, concussions, corneal abrasions, intestinal infections. Exposed nail bed pain is worse. It is worse partly because it's self-inflicted and therefore shameful but also because, being self-inflicted, the mind can't help but come up with rationalizations for the injury. Which would be useful, a sort of retrospective self-protection, if the mind in anxiety happened to be completely delusive. But because in anxiety the mind is only *half*-delusive, the non-delusive half immediately brands the rationalization (e.g., "Nail-biting is a valid form of grooming that's as old as the hominids, and that's what I was up to") as a rationalization without having any impact whatsoever on the delusive, rationalization-forming half of the mind, and this intrapsychic conflict (bear with me here) registers as a totalizing sense of humiliating self-ridiculousness. And then this totalizing sense of humiliating self-ridiculousness increases the pain signal.

This is all very perverse and recursive and hard enough to process when there's only one masticated finger. But it is the rare nail-biter who is so controlled. I started biting my nails after Esther, then stopped, then started again when I arrived at college. By the time I stood steeling myself to cross the no-man's-land separating me from the clinic, I had ten fingers whose nails I had gnawed clean, plus various and assorted nibbles, tears, gouges, and chew marks farther south. My hands looked as if they had been manicured with an immersion blender. In my first weeks away I wore Band-Aids, but in time the damage grew so extensive that to cover all the wounds I would have had to wear multiple bandages on every finger, which would almost certainly have raised an administrative red flag. So I wandered from class to class with my hands thrust into the pockets of my jeans, where the jagged nail edges and skin flaps attracted lint and crumbs and other detritus, or else got caught on stray threads, exacerbating the bleeding and intensifying the pain.

• • •

I checked my watch. There were exactly four minutes until the start of my session. In this part of campus, there were a lot of trees and large boulders. It was possible that someone was watching and judging me even now. Scanning the grounds, I thought I detected movement down by the athletic center. I'd have to work quickly if I was going to fool anyone.

I began with my posture. Of all the corrupted aspects of my body, it seemed like the easiest one to correct: stop slouching. But to my surprise, I found that I could no more stand straight than I could sprout wings and fly to therapy. Curiously, this was not because my spine disobeyed the command to straighten; it was because my mind refused to issue the command in the first place. My brain—my perplexed, worn-out brain—didn't want to budge. Wasn't going into work this morning. Was calling in sick. Sorry, kid, you're going to have to stay slumped today.

In the years since that moment, I've come to recognize this kind of mental intransigence as the second obstacle to acting calm when you are anxious. It is a problem that tends to progress the further into a spate of anxiety you get. The process is reminiscent of Stockholm syndrome: The longer the brain is exposed to anxiety's relentless messages of hopelessness and despair, the more convinced it becomes that those messages convey the ineluctable truth. This isn't surprising when you remember that the brain evolved to protect the organism against injury and death. The brain is good at pleasure; it likes orgasms, glucose, and companionship. But it is *exceptional* at fear. If the brain wasn't a first-class fear-monger, if it wasn't always ready and poised to pound on the alarm bells, then a threat to the organism might end the whole game before there was any chance to experience pleasure. In evolutionary terms, fear trumps all else.

Anxiety, though, is different from fear, and to understand why faking it can be so hard it's important to know just how they're different. Freud was of the opinion that in fear a person is responding to a specific and immediate threat to physical safety while in anxiety a person is responding to a threat that is objectless, directionless, and located somewhere far off in the future—ruination, for example, or humiliation, or decay. This was already the standard line in his day and it's still the standard line, for good reason. The distinction highlights the untethered quality of anxiety—what a contemporary of Freud's called the "meaning-less frenzy" of the experience. A current expert, the psychologist David Barlow, defines fear as "a primitive alarm in response to present danger, characterized by strong arousal and action ten-dencies." Anxiety is "a future-oriented emotion, characterized by perceptions of uncontrollability and unpredictability over poten-tially aversive events and a rapid shift in attention to the focus of potentially dangerous events or one's own affective response to those events." That last clause—"one's own affective response to those events"—is just a fancy way of saying that anxious people pay a lot of attention to their own anxiety.

And yet to talk about anxiety as directionless and formless and fear as focused and specific only says how the two experiences are different, not how they're related. It also suggests, in a back-handed way, that fear is normal, a hardwired Darwinian response, and that anxiety is abnormal, a sort of postindustrial, urban af-fliction. No experts say this outright, or even at all. Everyone acknowledges that anxiety is an ancient and ubiquitous emotion that only becomes abnormal when it is out of proportion to what-ever threatening event might—possibly, maybe—happen. Normal anxiety is a state of aroused preparedness. Abnormal anxiety is an overreaction.

For example, if you are camping out in an African animal preserve and you have trouble sleeping because you don't want to be eaten alive, you're normally anxious. If you're drinking beer at a bar in Fort Lauderdale and you're edgy because one day you might go off on a camping trip during which an animal will stroll into your tent and eat you alive, you need a prescription. Still, because the traditional line on fear and anxiety doesn't link the two up very well, anxiety comes off with an unmistakably clinical reputation.

Which is why I've come to prefer a newer view of fear and anxiety. This comes from the eminent psychiatrist Aaron Beck. Beck agrees that fear is more focused and fundamental than anxiety, but he changes the equation by emphasizing the mental rather than the physical basis of fear. By doing this he manages to get fear and anxiety under the same roof, namely the skull, and to connect them logically. Fear, Beck writes,

> is a primitive automatic neurophysiological state of alarm involv-
> ing the *cognitive appraisal* of imminent threat or danger to the
> safety and security of an individual. Anxiety is a complex cogni-
> tive, affective, physiological and behavioral response system (i.e.,
> *threat mode*) that is activated when anticipated events or cir-
> cumstances are deemed to be highly aversive because they are
> perceived to be unpredictable, uncontrollable events that could
> potentially threaten the vital interests of an individual.

Here's his plain-English version: "Fear is the appraisal of danger; anxiety is the unpleasant feeling state evoked when fear is stimu-lated."

This version of things goes far in explaining why I had such a hard time straightening out my back when I was standing at the start of the footpath to the clinic. In Beck's account, there are two main stages in the gestation of clinical anxiety. In the first stage, fear is stimulated—a threat is noticed—and an "unpleasant feeling state" is evoked. This is a hopeful time, relatively, because while the unpleasant feeling state is really and truly unpleasant, it's also new and unusual. It's not foreign: Everyone has experienced anxiety in situations where anxiety is warranted—while waiting for medical test results, for example. But the first time that you experience anxiety that has no obvious connection to a logical threat, in a situation in which the vast bulk of humanity would fail to respond with anxiety, you know it. It feels wrong. It feels off. It feels *crazy*. This is good. It means you still have a chance. This is the optimal time to hie thee to a therapist, the woods, an ashram. This is the time, before the great vindictive hand of Jehovah slams shut the gate, to dive back into Eden and cling tightly to a well-rooted tree. Because the gate *will* close. That's how the brain operates; it is frighteningly quick to form habits. And Beck's unpleasant feeling state is a self-perpetuating little bastard. Fear—of something, anything—calls it up and, jittery as it is genetically determined to be, it looks for other things to be scared of. It responds to fear by looking for fear, and the world being the world, it finds it. In this way, the merry-go-round of anxiety is fired up. The loop begins: fear to anxiety to fear to anxiety to fear to anxiety. This is the second stage and it is really hard to get out of.

It isn't impossible, however. There are ways to break the cycle. Most of these ways, of course, are laborious. They mean sitting down for months or years on end, fighting to alter the mental habits of a lifetime. In short, they mean therapy of one sort or another. But what if your mental habits are precisely what are keeping you from therapy? What if, like me, you are so anxious that you can't even move, let alone think rationally? How do you combat paralysis?

The strange answer I discovered that morning was . . . you just do. In dire situations, those in which obligation or desperation seem to leave you with no choice, you can still exercise your will. Like the Lorax at the end of the Dr. Seuss book, gripping the seat of his own pants and lofting himself into the sky, you retain within you the ability to wrench yourself out of your anxious state and into action, if only for a moment.

I almost gave up. I almost turned around and headed back for the dorm and Long Island. But as I was standing there, going to town on my nails with an especially compulsive fervor, I heard the sound of a car coming down the road, heading in my direction, and, motivated by the same fear of exposure that had been keeping me motionless, I forced myself to take a first step. Doing this meant engaging in an almost athletic way of thinking, in which I had to envision my conscious will as a sort of slothful, stupefied figure within my head. I envisioned this will of mine and I pretended it was my job to rouse him, to shake him alert so he could do the job I needed him to do. It was as though my will were one of those world-weary ex-cops in action movies whom the mayor turns to when the city is being tormented by unprecedentedly resourceful terrorists and what it needs desperately is a savior, any savior, even one with a bum knee, a five-day stubble, and no respect for authority.

Things didn't go well at first. As I took one step, then another, then another, calm was decidedly not the attitude projected. The attitude projected was more like acute lower-GI distress. Every muscle in my body felt leaden and rigor mortic.

Then, somehow, I found a groove. Which is to say, I found a pattern of movement I could ease into and sustain. My arms started to swing more lightly, my hips bobbed and swayed, my head straightened out on my neck. It was my first taste of the knowledge that this was possible, that the mechanics of my existence allowed for internal and external life to diverge so radically, and that I was able to manage it says something, I think, about the strangeness of the conscious will, which, short of finely calibrated pharmaceutical interventions, can only be activated by itself—like God summoning himself into existence. Not that my mind, as I made my way down the path, was on metaphysics. One of the things anxiety educates you in is how deeply *physical* thought can be, how concrete. In anxiety, there is no time to luxuriate in abstractions. It's just you and your mind, which has fists and is using them. It may be dualistic and logically untenable to posit the situation as You v. Head; it may not make sense philosophically. But in the throes of anxiety? In the cognitive shit? There's really no other way to think about what's going on.

The therapist was the only person I have ever seen outside of silent movies who stroked his beard to illustrate that he was thinking. He was slim and short and thirty at the oldest. His office, which I gathered he shared with several other fledgling shrinks, resembled the office of a teaching assistant in one of the university's less respected academic departments. It wasn't much larger than a tool shed, and not much neater. Tall piles of manila folders lay on a series of cheap aluminum shelves. Case notes,

I assumed—the life stories and weekly unravelings of the furtively afflicted. There was barely enough space in the room to fit the chairs on which we sat, facing each other. When the therapist hitched up his pants, our knees kissed.

"So what brings you here today?" he asked.

My heart fell. "What brings you here today?" It was such a hackneyed question, a line from a bad script. Couldn't he have done better than that? It didn't seem to bode well. Since he was only my second therapist, I didn't yet know that all therapeutic openings are hackneyed. There is no original way to ask a person why he is feeling unwell enough to seek help. Therapeutic openings always make me feel sorry for the therapist, who has the difficult job of having both to elicit the patient's history and difficulties and to establish an attitude of authoritative concern. "How can I help you?" "Tell me a bit about yourself." "What's bothering you?" Compared to the alternatives, "What brings you here today?" is actually pretty good: open-ended, present-tense, oriented toward the petitioner rather than the petition.

"I suffer from anxiety," I said, and then a stiff jolt of awareness struck me somewhere in my abdomen, for I'd never said it like that before. I'd never used the word in that kind of sentence. I'd used it, usually in adjectival form: "I'm feeling anxious." I knew, because I had looked it up, that Xanax was an "anxiolytic," and that the root of "anxiolytic" was "anxiety" (Latin *anxietas*: fretfulness). I knew that all the words that applied here and there to my experience—sadness, depression, nervousness, despair, dissociation, obsession, distraction, self-awareness, hysteria, angst, dejection—were satellites orbiting around the main word, the main event: anxiety. And yet there was something more than accuracy at play here. The setting made things more complicated than that. Saying "I suffer from anxiety" to a therapist changed the word from a descriptor to an act of acquiescence—a bowing to the authority of pathology.

Then I was surprised again by what the therapist did next. The poor man must have been as nervous as I was, because after nodding sympathetically for a few seconds he reached to a shelf behind him, pulled down a thick psychology textbook, and proceeded to flip through it. When he had found the page he was looking for he gave his beard a few languid strokes and read.

"Anxiety," he said. "Anxiety is a relatively permanent state of worry and nervousness occurring in a variety of mental disorders, usually accompanied by compulsive behavior or attacks of panic." He raised his eyes. "Is this what you've been feeling?" he asked. "Would you say this describes your experience accurately?"

I nodded. "Yes, I think so. I think that describes it."

He turned the page. His beard received further ministration.

"There's a table in here," he said. "A list of criteria that will help us determine whether what you're feeling is . . . well, whether it's a problem or not. I'm going to read these aloud to you. Is that all right?"

"Yes. OK."

"Here we go then," he said. "Number one. Would you say that you've been anxious more often than not for the past six months?"

"Uh, no. Not really. It's pretty new. Well this time it is. I've had it before. I've gone through it before. But this time it's only been for about a month, since school started. But it's been bad, really bad. Like, constant."

"So that's a 'no' then." He twisted over to his desk and scribbled a note. "That's good. That's a good sign. Let's go on to number two. Would you say you have difficulty controlling your worry?"

"Oh, yeah. Definitely. Yes."

He scribbled again. "Three. Please answer yes or no to the following symptoms. Do you feel restless, keyed up, or on edge?"

"Yes."

"Are you easily fatigued?"

"Yes."

"Do you have difficulty concentrating?"

"Yes."

"Are you irritable?"

"Yes."

"Do you feel any muscle tension?"

"Yes."

"And finally, do you have sleep disturbance?"

"Sleep disturbance?"

"Trouble getting to sleep, trouble staying asleep, unsatisfying sleep."

"Yes."

"Right, six out of six."

"Is that bad?"

He affected a neutral tone. "There's no good or bad here. We're just trying to determine what's troubling you. Now, then, question number four. . . . Well, four I can't really ask you. Four is a little technical. Let's move on to five. Would you say that your anxiety causes you impairment in social, occupational, or other important areas of functioning?"

I felt like I might cry if I spoke, so I nodded.

"Is that a yes?"

I nodded more vigorously. He made an empathy face. "I know this is hard. There's not much more."

I nodded.

"Six. Is your anxiety due to the direct physiological effects of medication, substance abuse, or a general medical condition such as hyperthyroidism, and is it exclusive of a mood disorder, a psychotic disorder, or . . . well, wait. I'm seeing now that this one might be hard for you to answer, too. So let's just—let's just skip it."

I started to cough, to beat back the tears.

"Maybe we should just"—he was thumbing through the book now as I coughed louder—"maybe the thing to do would be"—he flipped to the index, scanning it with one hand while with the other he played with his beard—"maybe we should just talk a little then."

"But do you think—"

"See where it takes us. Just discuss what you've been feeling."

"Do you think—"

"Hash it out."

"Do you think there's, like, something wrong with me?"

He leaned way back in his chair. Our knees touched again.

"Don't quote me on this," he said. "But I'd say there's definitely something off kilter."

10.

people of the book

I made my way back along the footpath and onto the campus proper. The session made the college seem even more foreign and forbidding than before. Walking into the shadow of the science complex, I recalled a statistic our guide had conveyed, inexplicably, on our campus tour. Each academic year at the university, she announced to the assembled families, more mice were decapitated for experiments than students graduated. I scrambled back into daylight.

Then, at the top of a hill leading to the Castle, an imposing medieval replica complete with turrets, corbels, buttresses, and battlements, I caught a sight through scattered oaks of the entrance to the library, and my mood improved. I hadn't been inside the library since my truncated attempt at therapeutic breathing; it had taken on, like a growing number of settings in my life, the queasy aura of my discomfort.

This now struck me as intensely stupid. The library: of course! The library was the solution to my predicament, the only conceivable place on campus I'd be able to find the solitude I needed and the wisdom I wanted. I had no intention of going back to the clinic. (I'd lie to my parents from then on.) What was the point? I could do better than some newly minted shrink just scanning the shelves, picking out clues and consolations when and from where it felt right to me. And *how* it felt right. With a therapist you have to sit and be prodded into self-examination no matter how anxious you are. With books you can shut the process down at any moment with the flip of a cover. If a book wasn't working for you, if you found it too offensive or contrary or pretentious or slight, you could simply choose another. Being in the library was like being in the perfect sanatorium. How could I not have realized this?

Well, I realized it now, and I let that realization lead me through the doors and past the thrumming, crowded computer stations. For the next four months, until winter break, I barely left the library's crypt-like lower levels.

Some months ago, my brother Scott e-mailed me a document along with a note that said, "Just thought you might like to see how it's shaking out." The document was titled thebookofscott .doc, and it consisted of about forty quotations organized into five "chapters": Discipline, Awareness, Fear, Creativity, and General Tonic. Scott had been accumulating the quotations for several months, ever since, in the same two-week period, his wife gave birth and he started a new job and he found that, once again, hypochondriasis was making life difficult to lead. His goal was to produce a compact volume of wisdom—a kind of commonplace book—that he could use to pull himself together whenever he felt his nerves growing frayed.

One motivation for the project was envy. My brothers and I grew up in a Jewish but largely secular home. Each of us had a bar mitzvah, but we managed to emerge from childhood with little understanding of, and littler faith in, religious texts. Scott is convinced that our lack of religion has handicapped us psychologically. "It's not really fair, when you think about it," he told me when he began the project. "We're surrounded by people who came into this world with these portable little bundles of certainty, these neat foundational texts. They don't have to go rooting around for comforting words. They were handed to them at birth—pre-edited, pre-legitimized, pre-authorized. There are almost seven billion people on the planet and ninety percent have scriptures. And what do we have? What did we get? Nothing. A handful of movies and a few of Dad's jokes. We're at sea. We've always been at sea."

It remains to be seen whether *The Book of Scott* will close the gap between my brother and the world's devout. Yet looking over its contents recently (Milton: "He who reigns within himself and rules his passions, desires, and fears, is more than a king." Santayana: "Let a man once overcome his selfish terror at his own finitude, and his finitude is, in one sense, overcome." Flaubert: "Shut up and get on with it.") I couldn't help but regret that I didn't have something like it to guide me during those long months I spent in the bowels of the college library. The qualities embodied by Scott's selections—simplicity, mindfulness, pragmatism, stoicism—are exactly those qualities an anxious person needs to foster in himself if he is going to change in any real and lasting way. They are the qualities common to every therapeutic literature that has ever been useful to anyone, and at the age of eighteen I didn't have the first clue they were what I should be searching for.

There are many sections in a library where an anxious young man might find solace and self-understanding: poetry, philosophy, theology, psychology, art. Being fond of stories, I gravitated toward the fiction stacks. I staked a claim to a carrel beside the Vs and Ws in twentieth-century American literature, in a dim corner of the first basement level, and between dutiful sessions attending to class assignments, I began to range at random through the offerings.

I found myself reading anything whose opening lines, scanned standing up in the narrow alleys between the shelves, felt capable of coaxing my anxiety down from its stubborn heights. Nabokov famously said that one should gauge literature with "the top of the tingling spine." I gauged it with the icicle in my chest. If, reading the first sentences of a novel, my icicle thawed, I would carry the book with me back to the carrel and jump in. If my icicle began to swell and stick in my sternum, I would slam the book shut and replace it on the shelf. In this way, the masterworks of modern American literature began to shake out according to a sort of ad hoc neurotic analysis. James, Faulkner, O'Connor, Cheever, DeLillo, Gaddis, and Pynchon were among those deemed, for whatever unconscious reasons, too anxiety-provoking to absorb. Those who made the cut included Hemingway, Bellow, Updike, Doctorow, and Styron. But the author whom my icicle urged me to read more avidly than any other that year, the author who, once I discovered him, seemed to articulate my condition with such uncanny precision that his novels came to be not just a comfort but an explanation—a diagnostic source—was Philip Roth. When I found Roth, I felt I had found my anxiety's Rosetta Stone.

The affinity was immediate. The first Roth book I pulled from the shelf was *The Ghost Writer*, his eighth. It was like looking into a mirror. Here, making his inaugural appearance, was Nathan

Zuckerman—Roth's "alter-consciousness," as he has fastidiously called his creation—and he was just like me: a bookish, sensitive, libidinous young man trying to make his way following a cloistered childhood in a loving Jewish home. No, change that: trying to make his way *in spite of* a cloistered childhood in a loving Jewish home. For that was the conflict, the stark, startling, surprisingly resonant conflict at the core of the novel. Zuckerman, just a few years removed from being "an orthodox college atheist and highbrow-in-training," has written a story based on an embarrassing episode in his family's past and finds himself, suddenly and for the first time, the object of his parents' disapproval. Ambitious, passionate, idealistic to a fault, he has set out to exert his will on the world and discovered that he is more bound than he had ever imagined to the concern, authority, and love—above all the love, to which he has an "addiction"—of his formidable, doting family.

In its particulars, Zuckerman's story was not mine. I could scarcely imagine undergoing a bruising battle with my father, as he does, over the competing claims of literary integrity and ethnic solidarity. My father would probably take literature's side. But it *felt* like my story. The novel excavated a species of torment—a concurrent hunger and repulsion for the protection and adoration of one's family—that I had never encountered in a novel before, and to which I felt a curious, reflexive kinship. After I read *The Ghost Writer* (twice) I turned at once to Roth's other books, and as I inhaled them in order that fall, from *Goodbye, Columbus* to *Operation Shylock,* I came again and again upon the same dogged theme, the same irresolvable tension, and I began to work up a theory as to why Roth's depiction of family life felt so familiar.

•   •   •

The big clue came from brooding about my surroundings. Whenever I dared to voyage away from my carrel and out of the basement—furtive, blinking sorties to stretch my legs—I would look out the tall windows at the campus and think, *I don't want to be here.* I had never wanted to be here. I hated it here. Yet I was here. Why on earth was I here?

It was my mother, I recalled, who first suggested that I consider Brandeis, at the start of my senior year. The idea struck me as preposterous. College, I explained, was for broadening one's perspectives, for seeking out the unfamiliar and the untried. It should be, ideally, like the black-and-white-to-Technicolor switchover in *The Wizard of Oz.* Brandeis's student body was nearly two-thirds Jewish, just like my high school. If I were being raised in, say, the Ozarks, it might make sense to enroll, see what it's like to be in the majority for a change. But I was being raised on Long Island. I was swimming in Jews. Every third friend a Rachel or an Aaron, a bar or bat mitzvah every weekend, High Holiday services so crowded people scalped tickets. "Ma," I said, "we've got two black families in this town and one of them goes to our synagogue. What's the point?"

But she persisted. She appealed to my practical side. I needed to increase the number of my applications. I needed to apply to more schools likely to offer me scholarship money. I needed another safety school. Then the coup de grâce: What was the big deal? Why all the fuss? If I got in and didn't want to go, I wouldn't go.

"Humor me," she said. "Fill out an application."

I humored her. By that time, my anxiety had subsided to the point at which I could appreciate humor again. Kierkegaard, I would later learn, argued that there is an inverse relationship between humor and anxiety, since humor comes out of taking a detached stance toward something and anxiety is the state of being utterly, hopelessly attached to everything. One of the things I knew about Brandeis was a sort of joke. Originally, the school was to have been named Einstein University, but when the founders suggested this to the great man, in the 1930s, he demurred. That's very thoughtful of you, he said, but my life isn't over. What if I do something bad? What if my work turns out to be, you know . . . destructive? Not long afterward, Einstein urged Roosevelt to build the atomic bomb. "The worst mistake of my life," he later called it. Ha ha.

When the university sent its acceptance package, it was accompanied by the offer of a full scholarship. I wouldn't have to pay a nickel. This was very flattering, but I wasn't prepared for how the money would transform, in my mother's hands, from a financial incentive into an emotional one. My high school was one of those suburban piles crammed to the rafters with overachievers—dozens upon dozens of extracurricularly resplendent teenagers with secret amphetamine habits and early-onset gastric ulcers. I rated, but just barely, and I'd never much cared. Now came the suggestion that I *should* care, that to have had so many above me in the rankings for so long could only have been a strain on my confidence, which was, as evidenced by my recent breakdown, lacking. The scholarship Brandeis was offering was an opportunity to rise in my own and others' estimations, to bolster my self-esteem. It was an opportunity, as my mother telegraphed all this, to be "a big fish in a small pond."

This argument confused me on a number of levels. To begin with, I hadn't thought my self-esteem needed so heavy an infusion. It's true that I'd gone through a tough time. But I was on the upswing. Also, I had not previously harbored an ambition to be a "big fish." An engaged fish, yes. An involved fish. But dominant?

It honestly never occurred to me. Finally, this wasn't just any small pond. This was a Jewish small pond. Which suggested that there were certain ethnic and religious considerations at play in my mother's mind. This was odd, because I'd never thought my parents cared much about the maintenance or advancement of our Jewish identities beyond what was required as a matter of social and familial course: five or six desultory years of Hebrew school; a lavish bar mitzvah with hired dancers and a Viennese table; an annual seder in which the epic tale of exile, exodus, and Egyptian infanticide was speed-read so that we could get down to the real business of engorging ourselves on brisket. I thought all the Jewish stuff was just so much inherited furniture. But for my mother, it now seemed, it meant enough that she was troubled by the thought of its absence in my life. A few weeks later, touring Georgetown, by whose Gothic spires and Jesuit gravitas I was particularly entranced, my mother took a long look around and said, "All these crosses make me uncomfortable!" Then she asked the tour guide where the Hillel chapter was located.

A more self-assured young man would not have been swayed by any of this. A more self-assured young man would have gone and done exactly what he wanted where he wanted. But that was just the point, I realized. That was the most plausible answer to the question I wanted answered—not just "What am I doing here?" but the exponentially more consequential "What's wrong with me?" What defect was responsible for this terrible anxiety?

What defect? How about being a weakling? How about being a pushover? How about being shamefully, contemptibly, pathetically, unreservedly acquiescent to the wills of others? How about being so weak of will that you may as well not even have one?

It fit, this explanation. It fit as an explanation for why I'd enrolled at Brandeis despite not wanting to, it fit as an explanation for why I'd slept with Esther despite not wanting to, and it fit as an explanation for why I'd broken down in the aftermath of both: Even someone who acquiesces in ignorance knows in his bones that he has acquiesced. His body registers the self-betraying act of submission. And I never acquiesced in ignorance. Never. Whenever I did what I didn't want to do I did it with a glimmer of awareness, with an intuition of my own desires but with a slavish readiness to abandon that intuition. At moments of decision I treated my intuition in the opposite way everyone treated theirs, not as a handy volitional dispatch from the characterological depths but as a suspicious, mercurial, dubious voice from the same, mired in the chaos of existence and so best to be discounted in favor of more objective-seeming data—namely, other people's opinions. I shut my eyes, held out my hands, and asked other people to lead me. What else could I possibly be but anxious?

I didn't blame my mother for my feeble will, though. Don't get me wrong. Despite the torrid Oedipal rants of *Portnoy's Complaint*, which had me cackling with pleasure, that wasn't the lesson about anxiety I took away from my reading. I didn't emerge from those stacks poisoned by grievances against a castrating mother, that mythical villain. On the contrary, I emerged from the library more sympathetic to my mother than ever, more cognizant and welcoming of our similarities, and even with a wry smile for where our little collegiate psychodrama had landed me. It was perfect, in its way. My anxious mother had contrived to deliver her anxious son to the land of the anxious: to the Jews. Because of Roth, I could now appreciate the joke.

Because of Roth, I had to appreciate the joke. Appreciating

the joke was the only viable prescription for the diagnosis his books amounted to, and what they amounted to was this: anxiety was my birthright. This wasn't panic disorder or generalized anxiety disorder or any other *DSM* designation. This was a *Jewish* disorder—a genetic and environmental disease that consists of being pulled simultaneously in the directions of rebellion and approval-seeking, of wanting to live adventurously and wanting to live conventionally, of selfishness and selflessness. This thing I was walking around with wasn't psychiatric; it was ethnic, like Tay-Sachs or a taste for smoked fish. And if I was reading Roth correctly, it was untreatable.

It was a relief. I felt relief having drawn this conclusion. It lent my anxiety a sheen of, if not normality then at least of sanctioned abnormality. It gave the condition a kind of tribal distinction, a historical heft and respectability. I was aware, in no small part because Roth's novels fixated on the point, that not everyone felt the same way. Poor Zuckerman, like his creator, suffers the disdain of many of his own people for publishing books that portray Jews in an unflattering light. ("Dear Mr. Zuckerman: It is hardly possible to write of Jews with more bile and contempt and hatred. . . .") The last word Zuckerman's own father speaks before he dies, staring into his son's eyes, is: "Bastard." And at the end of *Portnoy,* Roth cleverly subjects his protagonist to the scorn of his exact opposite—a courageous, decisive, morally resolute Israeli soldier.

By dawn I had been made to understand that I was the epitome of what was most shameful in "the culture of the Diaspora." Those centuries and centuries of homelessness had produced just such disagreeable men as myself—frightened, defensive, self-deprecating, unmanned and corrupted by life in the gentile world. It was Diaspora Jews just like myself who had gone by the millions to the gas chambers without ever raising a hand against their persecutors, who did not know enough to defend their lives with their blood. The Diaspora! The very word made her furious.

Yet for all the disparagement, no one inside or outside Roth's fictional world denied that such frightened, self-deprecating, disagreeably overwrought Jews existed. How could they? We were here. We were real. *I* was real. My mother was real. My brother Scott was real. Woody Allen and Jules Feiffer and Fran Lebowitz were real. Those centuries and centuries of homelessness had taken place, and what Roth's fiction seemed at least in part designed to argue was that the ceaseless cerebration in which two millennia of Jewish wandering had allegedly resulted was not only valid but vital. Exegesis—interminable, serpentine, mind-knotting, tormented exegesis—was the very soul of the Jewish experience. The goys read the Bible and only the Bible. The Jews read the Torah and what thousands of long-dead, contentious, slippery-minded scholars had to say about what the Torah may or may not mean, what to do when it seems to mean two different things at once, what seeming to mean two different things at once says about meaning in general and about what God may or may not be trying to say about meaning in general, and about how all this should or should not color one's understanding of divine authority, ethics, secular law, and so on and so forth in an unending welter of confusion. This is Judaism. This disputatiousness was the engine of its development. And like it or not this, Roth seemed to be saying, is part of its psychic legacy. In "Eli, the Fanatic," one of his earliest stories, a young, assimilated suburban lawyer is enlisted to evict the tenants of a Hasidic yeshiva that has sprouted up in the neighborhood and ends up wearing the uniform of the chief rabbi, wide-brimmed hat, phylacteries, and all. Everyone thinks Eli has had a nervous breakdown, but, Roth writes, "he felt those black clothes as if they were the skin of his skin . . . he would walk forever in that black suit, as adults whispered of his strangeness and children made 'Shame . . . shame' with their fingers."

That defiance in the face of shame was perhaps the greatest attraction of Roth's work. Roth's protagonists are for the most part not good men. They tend to be selfish, overbearing, misogynistic, and vain. In some instances they are downright vicious. But they are almost always exceedingly honest—even, or especially, at the expense of their own serenity. They never recoil from the truth, even when the truth is horrendous. Their will to self-awareness is almost tyrannical.

This thrilled me. I exalted in the uncompromising nature of Roth's characters, for they seemed to transform the idea of anxiety from a pathology into nothing less than a virtue—a heroic trait. They suffered, Roth's men. How they suffered! But their suffering was indivisible from their brilliance. They refused to sacrifice even one mote of their intelligence for the sake of dumb, ordinary comfort. In this Roth is like Kierkegaard, and not yet knowing the risks I attended closely to the message: To be anxious wasn't shameful, it was a high calling. It was to be alive to life's contradictions, more receptive to the true nature of things than everyone else. It was to be a person who saw with sharper eyes and felt with more active skin. It was to be a writer, and I wanted in.

episode three

11.

the facts

Here are some of the jobs an anxiety sufferer should, if he is the slightest bit sensible, avoid at all costs: high-security prison guard, coal miner, neurosurgeon, offshore oil rig worker, Mafia henchman, CIA field operative, investigative journalist in Moscow, criminal court judge in Bogotá, drug enforcement agent in Tijuana, rickshaw driver in New Delhi, political cartoonist in Pyongyang, and the opposition leader of any Central African nation.

Here is another: fact-checker at a major American magazine.

Indeed, just as the law wisely prohibits minors from working in factories and the blind from working as air-traffic controllers, it should prohibit the anxious from working as fact-checkers. This is because fact-checking subsists on an ideal—perfection—that is also the petty demon that haunts the anxious mind. The salient word is "petty." The jobs listed above all consist of life-or-death decision-making; the vigilance they demand is warranted by the high stakes. In a state of anxiety, a person is as vigilant as any surgeon or spy but without the surgeon's or spy's cause to be vigilant. The energy put in is all out of proportion to the actual threat.

The fact-checker's job is to inspect the factual content of the magazine that employs him. Depending on the magazine, this content may take the form of anything from gossip item to investigative report to book review to short story. What doesn't vary from publication to publication is what the checker spends his days inspecting for. He spends his days inspecting for error. Error of any and every possible kind—small, large, technical, logical, expository, dialogical, unwitting, nefarious, academic, essential, graphical, punctuational, typographical, attributional—is the only thing the checker thinks or cares about from the moment he sits at his desk in the morning to the moment he gets up at the end of the day. His paycheck depends exclusively on his ability to scrutinize the fruits of other people's labor for bruises, blemishes, and rot. This task often results in an unfortunate mindset. To the journalist being subjected to a rigorous checking process, the checker is a relentless detective, dissecting and probing every niggling point. Yet it is the checker who actually has the psychology of the persecuted, for he lives in unceasing terror of failure. His professional standing and his self-esteem demand that he be on constant alert against slippage and distraction. Being a fact-checker is like playing the classic videogame *Kaboom!,* in which you have to move laterally back and forth trying to catch little cartoon bombs as they fall from the top of the screen, speeding up, slowing down, increasing and decreasing in frequency, but never stopping, always falling, brooking no error or else it's *KABOOM!* Game over.

Sara Lippincott, a former fact-checker, has said that when an error sneaks into print in any journal of reputation, it "live[s] on and on in libraries carefully catalogued, scrupulously indexed . . . silicon-chipped, deceiving researcher after researcher down through the ages, all of whom will make new errors on the strength of the original errors, and so on and on into an exponential explosion of errata."

An exponential explosion of errata. By now the reader will recognize this phrase as pretty much a precise rendering of how my anxiety works its clockwork horrors. Its default setting is the perpetual, paralytic awareness that even the most mundane decision can be the fulcrum on which fate turns and Armageddon is permitted to dawn. When I die my epitaph will read: HERE LIES DANIEL SMITH. HE LIVED IN FEAR OF AN EXPONENTIAL EXPLOSION OF ERRATA.

The magazine Sara Lippincott worked for was *The New Yorker. The New Yorker* invented the modern fact-checking system. Then they exported it, forever changing American journalism. One of the magazines to which *The New Yorker* exported its system of fact-checking was *The Atlantic Monthly.* This was a hand-to-hand export, like Cortez introducing smallpox to the New World. In 1980, William Whitworth, a high-placed editor at *The New Yorker,* became editor in chief of *The Atlantic. The Atlantic* had only the most rudimentary fact-checking system. Whitworth quickly remedied this, calling in a veteran *New Yorker* checker to turn *The Atlantic* into a lean, ruthless, mistake-catching machine. Nineteen years later, right out of college, I was hired to be a staff editor at *The Atlantic.* At *The Atlantic,* "staff editor" usually meant "fact-checker."

For a young man of my literary ambitions and Semitic background, the appeal of *The Atlantic,* one of the oldest and most venerable of American magazines, was enormous. When I arrived, the magazine's editorial offices were located on the fifth floor of a converted warehouse in the North End. Riding the steel elevator each morning was like ascending to the summit of some

Brahmin Mount Olympus. The first sight to greet you when you approached the magazine's entrance was a large sepia-toned reproduction of the first page of the magazine's first issue, dated November 1857, at the center of which was a seventeenth-century woodcut portrait of John Winthrop, first governor of the Massachusetts Bay Colony and coiner of the phrase "city upon a hill." The second sight to greet you, when you walked through the door, was a framed drawing by the cartoonist Edward Sorel of three of *The Atlantic*'s founders toasting the editor and novelist William Dean Howells at a legendary dinner that took place in 1860 at Boston's Parker House hotel. Howells was twenty-three at the time, just two years older than I was then, and he had traveled from his hometown in eastern Ohio—a "devout young pilgrim from the West," as he would later put it—for no better reason than to lay his eyes on the "New England luminaries" of the American Renaissance, then in full swing. He also hoped, of course, that the luminaries would lay their eyes on him. Sorel's drawing commemorates the wild fulfillment of his hopes. Toasting the young Howells in the picture are three of the most esteemed and powerful cultural figures of the period: Oliver Wendell Holmes, celebrated essayist, wit, teacher, and inventor; James Russell Lowell, poet, critic, satirist, and *The Atlantic*'s first editor; and James T. Fields, the publisher of everyone from Tennyson and Thackeray to Emerson and Hawthorne and the owner of what was arguably the coolest beard in antebellum America. (Howells: It "flowed from his throat in Homeric curls.") The dinner was the first of Howells' life to be served in courses, and the first in which he was exposed to the way the comfortably elite spoke around each other.

"Well, James," Holmes said to Lowell as they all sat down, "this is something like the apostolic succession; this is the laying on of hands."

I didn't need any laying on of hands to feel that I too had at last been admitted to what Howells called "the fine air of high literature." The evidence was overwhelming. A hundred-and-forty-two years into its existence, *The Atlantic* no longer referred to its authors and editors by all three of their given names. So far as I could tell, that was pretty much the only change that had been carried out since Lee surrendered at Appomattox. The place hummed with old-school Yankee propriety—which is to say, it didn't hum at all. Business was conducted in a genteel hush, in closed-door isolation or quiet consultation at a tall table that was referred to, after the ancient Greeks, as the "agora." And all editorial comments and alterations were made on paper. In 1999! On actual, physical, pulped, pressed, and dried paper! As if every newspaper and magazine and one-man literary journal on the planet weren't already making the leap into digital editing. As if technological innovation had been frozen somewhere around V-E Day.

The place was a marvel of decorum and self-assurance. It was everything I wanted. The magazine felt like home, in the best sense of that word—a place of refuge, comfort, and well-being, a lap my mind wanted to nestle into and fall asleep in. My mind desperately needed this very home; I was convinced of that. Over the past three years I'd come to detect a simple, distressing pattern to how my anxiety waxed and waned. At school, in Massachusetts, it was ever-present but tolerable; at home, on Long Island, it was ever-present and all-consuming. Every holiday, without fail, the same transformation took place. Driving across the Throgs Neck Bridge; pulling into Port Authority on the twilight-dim Greyhound; thudding down on the tarmac on the Logan–LaGuardia shuttle; peering up at the schedule board at Penn Station as it flipped through all the characters in its guts, waiting for news of the train that would carry me east through all the stations whose names I'd heard the conductor intone so many times (Woodside, Jamaica, Hillside Facility, New Hyde Park, Merillon Avenue, Mineola, Carle Place, Westbury, Hicksville) it was like a prayer—no matter how I traveled the trip's last leg caused my ribs to grow cold and my mind frantic and I'd descend into a haze of anxiety that would only lift when I had returned north, weeks or months later. At first I blamed the encroaching idleness, which is as much anxiety's plaything as the devil's. Then I blamed the seasons—the depths of winter and the heights of summer just happening to be the conditions under which my anxiety flourished. Before long, however, I had drawn the obvious conclusion: the culprit was home itself. The atmosphere there exacerbated my anxiety as predictably as smog exacerbates asthma.

The response I am talking about is not simply a matter of regression, though that was certainly part of it—the well-known syndrome wherein returning home causes the adult psyche, and in particular the adult Jewish psyche, to revert to an earlier stage of development. (Portnoy: "Good Christ, a Jewish man with parents alive is a fifteen-year-old boy. . . . Did I say fifteen? Excuse me, I meant ten! I meant five! I meant zero! A Jewish man with his parents alive is half the time a helpless *infant!*") It was more conscious than that. By now I'd learned that to control my anxiety I needed controlled surroundings. A sturdy exterior was the best bulwark against a disordered interior. And home, as anyone could see, was not a controlled surrounding. With my mother in charge, it was more like a carnival—boisterous, sensational, diverting, filled with noise and energy—and it undid all my efforts at self-improvement. When I finally returned to school in mid-January or late August I felt like a bowl of Jell-O that had been taken out of the refrigerator too soon.

I wasn't asking for much, you see. I wasn't aiming high. I just wanted to be a nice cold bowl of Jell-O.

In addition to having the hush of a reading room, *The Atlantic's* offices were physically library-like, the walls lined with leather-bound volumes of back issues, books on travel and science and history and cuisine, and reference material of every kind imaginable. After hours I loved to tour the premises, browsing.

The best place to browse was a windowless room off the main hallway, where a horseshoe of aluminum filing cabinets housed the past several decades of the magazine's correspondence—breezy salvos between powerful editors and boldface-named authors. "Dear Ms. Oates . . ." "Dear Mr. Naipaul . . ." "Dear Mr. Bellow . . ." "Dear Mr. Nabokov . . ." On a dusty, tattered old couch crammed between the cabinets and an IBM Selectric I'd sit and read folder after folder, rapt. The one folder whose contents I read repeatedly, and with the furtive delight of a Peeping Tom, was labeled ROTH, PHILIP. Like his novels and stories, Roth's correspondence gave the impression of an uncompromising, fierce mind at work.

The folder contained almost twenty years' worth of exchanges between the author and William Whitworth, much of it concerning some freelance work Roth was quietly doing for the magazine, evaluating manuscripts. Roth's evaluations were always to the point: "I would have liked for that essay to be good," he wrote, "but it isn't." Often they were funny: "I don't like stories about kids who say 'Jesus' at the end of a paragraph." Sometimes he allowed himself a bit of personal grousing: "I'm feeling a little like a beached whale at the moment. Waiting for the tide to rise and wash me out to where the water is deep." Sometimes he boasted: "Too bad you couldn't come to the reading—had 'em hanging from the rafters." Sometimes, as in this, from the summer of 1993, he despaired: "Things stink, don't they? I've been very depressed by Janet Malcolm's case, as I think I may have told you, and even more depressed by Bill Clinton's case."

Then, in 1995, *The Atlantic*'s chief literary critic, an ancient, forbidding dowager who wore fur hats and smoked cigarillos, dismissed Roth's most recent and most ambitious novel, *Sabbath's Theater*, in two haughty lines: "As a protest against inevitable death, sexual excess is as futile as any other. Mr. Roth's latest novel makes it tiresome as well." Roth fired off an arctic display of wounded pride, excoriating Whitworth for having "abrogated" his duty as an editor in allowing the review to be published.

Whitworth's response was a model of pacification. He expressed sincere regret, but not remorse. He explained that he could correct his writers' grammar, or stop them from insulting racial and ethnic groups, but "I can't tell them what to think." He rehearsed the magazine's admiring critical record in regard to Roth's work, which, he added, he valued "above that of any other contemporary novelist." A few years pass, and the correspondence resumes on its old, friendly course.

I found all this exactly as it should be. The Jewish writer sputtered, pouted, and raged; the *goyische* magazine kept its head. The *goyische* magazine always kept its head. Being able to keep one's head was what it meant to be *goyische,* and what made *The Atlantic* seem as if it could only be a salutary place for a young man of my sensibility—a corrective institution. Even when the reserve displayed at the magazine was intimidating, I tried to take it as a useful lesson in how to live with less fear and trembling—how to conceal emotion and, through concealing, how to feel it less.

And sometimes it was intimidating. Not a month after being

hired, I was working in my office when all of a sudden I saw the figure of a man reflected in my computer screen. I swiveled my chair to find Whitworth in my doorway. He was a thin, striking man, with a shiny head ringed with gray and a thick beard like his nineteenth-century predecessors. He wore a bowtie and a three-piece suit that hung in folds off his frame. I'd never met him before.

"Hello," he said.

"Hello."

"I'm Bill."

I indicated that this was information I already possessed.

"I'd like to ask you a question," he said. Whitworth was from Little Rock and had a mellifluous Southern drawl. He'd covered the civil rights movement for the *New York Herald Tribune* and written profiles for *The New Yorker*. I was in awe of him. "I'm asking this question of some of the younger staff members."

"All right," I said, and steeled myself.

For a long while he just looked at his shoes, as if there were something written on them. Finally, he lifted his eyes and said, "So, who would you say is responsible for the Holocaust?"

The Holocaust! I can honestly say I hadn't expected that subject to come up. I don't know what I'd expected. A point of grammar, perhaps. Something about literature or science or youth culture. But the *Holocaust*? Why in God's name was he asking me about the Holocaust? All of a sudden a wave of paranoia I'd never experienced swept over me. Was he asking me about the Holocaust because I was a . . . could it be that . . . I mean, was he really asking others? Was he asking the gentiles? I was the only Jew under forty in the place, and it wasn't exactly like I passed. Could it be that—

That's when I remembered. The magazine was preparing a

cover story about the London libel trial that pitted David Irving, the military historian and Holocaust denier, against the scholar Deborah Lipstadt. It was a long, complicated article that dealt as much with the details and collective memory of the Final Solution as with the vagaries of English libel law. Whitworth *was* consulting me about youth culture, in a way. He wanted to know what a young person knew and thought about the Holocaust.

"Well," I said, aiming to impress, "there are of course conflicting views on that. For all the controversy stirred up by Daniel Goldhagen's book, which I personally found overwritten, his thesis that the Holocaust was the result of a strain of so-called eliminationist anti-Semitism in the German population itself is at least worthy of debate. So, too, are the arguments about Allied and especially American indifference to the fate of European Jewry. Painful as it is to consider, let alone talk about, I also think it's important to mention the inability of most European Jews, in particular those in Austria and Poland, to recognize the scope of the Nazi threat sooner and, when they did recognize it, to resist more violently. Of course, if you really want to get at the root of the tragedy you have to contend with the economic brutality of the Treaty of Versailles. I mean, I understand the impulse to hold the Kaiser accountable to the—"

"No," he said. "That's not what I mean. I mean specifically."

"Specifically?"

"Who *specifically* would you say was responsible for the Holocaust?"

I made the face children make when they can't tell if they're being toyed with or not. Whitworth's own expression offered no guidance.

"Um," I said, and then again: "Um . . . Adolf Hitler?"

He nodded. He seemed pleased. "OK," he said. "Thanks for

your help." Then he walked away, the only trace of him the reced-
ing clatter of his pocket change and the pounding of my heart.

For many minutes afterward I berated myself. *Adolf* Hitler?
Really? Had it really been necessary to include the man's first
name? What other Hitler could I have meant? Chuck Hitler?
Murray Hitler? Samantha Hitler? "Ah, Hitler you say, but which
one?" Once I'd muddled through the obligatory self-lacerations,
though, I began to see that there just might be a therapeutic
example for me in the exchange. Clearly some concern, some
spark of worry, had brought Whitworth to my door; he came
out of his office too rarely for it not to mean something. His
concern, I supposed, was that the name Hitler wouldn't resonate
as deeply with my generation of readers as it did with others,
that we wouldn't quite get it, or if we did get it that we wouldn't
quite care. If this was true it qualifies, I submit, as a fairly
neurotic concern. This was Hitler we were talking about, not
Bing Crosby; the resonance doesn't vary from generation to generation. Nonetheless, the important thing was that Whitworth
hadn't exposed his concern. He didn't blurt it out or try to justify
it. Nor did he dismiss it or stifle it. He addressed it in a straightforward, practical way. He thought to himself, "I have a nagging
worry. What's the best way to neutralize it?" Then he identified
that way and carried it out.

Et voilà! No more concern.

The more I considered his approach, the wiser it seemed. The
more I considered it, the more it also seemed redolent of the job
for which I had been hired. What had Whitworth done, after all,
but fact-check his worry? He'd acted according to the very principle I was then being trained to apply to the magazine's manuscripts and galleys: that there is no problem for which there isn't a
solution, so long as you know where and how to look. Logic. That

was the guiding idea, and at that early stage in my tenure it still seemed to hold great therapeutic promise.

The whole checking process seemed to hold therapeutic promise. The way I was being trained, the first step the fact-checker took when he was assigned an article was to go methodically through the piece and draw a straight line beneath anything that gave off even a whiff of factuality: names, dates, numerical figures, physical descriptions, job titles, anecdotes, quotations, photo credits . . . anything. As often as not, the result was a document in which nearly every word was underlined. But the process dictated that the checker not be daunted by this sight. The process dictated that the checker proceed in as orderly a manner as possible—either sequentially, if the piece allowed it, or by color-coding the facts according to their reputed sources and working through the colors one by one. Every time the checker confirmed a fact he was to draw a single, neat slash mark through it.

The first step in confirming a fact was to determine the most efficient method of investigation. Even in the pre-Google days, this could be very simple. That the Magna Carta was issued in 1215 is a fact that can be found in any dictionary. Usually, however, there was more work involved: getting in touch with sources, reading interview transcripts and newspaper articles, tracking down obscure reference materials. Sometimes there would be no clear answer at all, in which case a bit of creativity was in order. For example, one of the first pieces I was assigned to check was an essay by a young poet about a stretch of time he'd spent as a long-haul truck driver. Toward the end of the essay, the poet described the best roadside places along his route to urinate: "In Alabama exit 318 on the southbound [I-65] is a gem. The ramp cuts into a rock face that rises twenty feet above the shoulder, clung to by daring pine trees and vines with orange flowers. Crickets chirp."

By consulting a road atlas in *The Atlantic*'s library, I was able to confirm that there is in fact an exit 318 on the southbound I-65 and that the exit is in Alabama—Falkville, Alabama, to be precise, approximately fifty miles south of the Tennessee border. That crickets were chirping on one or all of the nights on which the poet emptied his bladder I could not confirm; that is the kind of assertion beside which a checker is permitted to make the notation "on au."—short for "on author." But I was able to confirm, with the help of a twenty-five-year-old article in *The Florida Entomologist* ("A Morphological Key to Field Crickets of Southeastern United States"), that the common southeastern field cricket, *Gryllus rubens*, does indeed flourish loudly in that part of Alabama. The obstacles I faced lay between these facts. How could I possibly verify, sitting as I was at a desk in Boston, that an interstate off-ramp 1,200 miles away cut into a twenty-foot-high rock face clung to by evergreens and orange-flowering vines? On the day before the issue was to close, the sentence was the last one standing. At last I took a deep breath and found the number for the Falkville police department. An amused sergeant listened as I explained my plight and then sent an officer out to look at the foliage.

This was an instance in which the facts as written checked out. When they didn't the checker was compelled to follow up by proposing a solution to the author. In some instances (rare, but they did happen) the assertion would be patently false; for example, Columbus sailed to America in 1493, FDR's first secretary of state was Shecky Greene, Wilt Chamberlain is a homosexual. These cases leave no room for argument. The author would have no choice but to submit to reality. Much more common were those cases in which reality itself was subject to dispute. Direct quotations were notorious in this regard. When calling a source a checker would often find that, rather than happily acceding to the wording as written, the source would deny, dispute, squirm, complain, and threaten, and that, when confronted with such resistance, the journalist would become ornery, insulted, and recalcitrant. In these cases, the checker's job is to play something like the role of the judge in *Kramer vs. Kramer.* The goal is to seek a fair settlement that redounds to the health of the child. You don't want either side getting what they're not supposed to get or losing what they're not supposed to lose. All you want is to know where reality lies, and to establish that you have to remain as level-headed as possible. You have to be cool, clinical, and detached—a sort of scientist of journalism. You have to be able to shut off the emotion, both yours and others', and focus on the evidence. Nothing but the evidence.

In a 2009 *New Yorker* essay, John McPhee wrote that it is characteristic of fact-checkers to be "calmer than marble." This is incorrect. Checkers are no less nervous than any other people. On average they may even be more nervous. Amy Meeker, a former head of *The Atlantic's* checking department, says that all checkers "need a certain amount of anxiety to do the job well." What she means is that fact-checking requires alertness, and anxiety fosters this.

The psychological problem the anxious checker faces is that the small amount of anxiety he needs to do the job well tends, in the hothouse of the work, to bloom, overshadowing and smothering the work's potential benefits. Learning to address concerns methodically, with reference to logic and empirical evidence, is one of the most useful things an anxious person can do. But it is a skill best learned, at least at first, in a pressureless environment. And fact-checking is never pressureless. Even at Whitworth's *Atlantic,* with its stately, salon-like atmosphere, the pressures were many and potent.

There was time pressure, of course. Even before you set a straight edge beneath an article's first fact, you know the clock is spinning down, time marching off to the brink. Fact-checkers become very attuned very quickly to the magazine's production schedule. They become attuned, also, to how time can change its pace according to one's mindset. In his essay, McPhee also wrote, "In one's head . . . things speed up in the ultimate hours." On this he's correct. More than twenty years after checking an article about Central America, Meeker can still remember jolting awake in bed at 3 a.m. the day before closing, the names of Salvadoran villages racing through her head.

Even worse than the time pressure is the social pressure. On the whole, writers are as anxious as fact-checkers, if not more so. Contrary to popular belief, however, they have less anxiety-provoking jobs. Once a reporter has informed a subject of what he is writing about, he often can conduct an interview in almost total silence and still get all the information he needs. Checkers don't have this luxury. Checkers always have to engage people actively—people whom they did not choose to engage and who very often have no interest in being engaged. When you're anxious, this is excruciating, for as an anxious person you have a supersensory ability to detect judgments—false judgments, but still—in the coughs, tics, throat-clearings, sniffs, pauses, ums, ahs, likes, and let's sees that occur in all normal conversations. And fact-checking entails a lot of conversation, almost always with strangers.

At the risk of presenting *The Atlantic*'s content at the time I worked there as inordinately urinary, here is an example. In late 1999, I had to call the Icelandic Phallological Museum—a museum about penises—to check a series of facts about the institution that appeared in a travel essay by Cullen Murphy, the magazine's managing editor. While confirming with the curator, one Sigurdur

Hjartarson, that his museum did in fact have on display the penises of all Icelandic mammals excluding man and a single species of whale,* I all of a sudden fell into a twisted tunnel of anxiety. First, going on nothing but the exuberance in Hjartarson's voice, I became certain that he was interpreting the tension in my own voice as disapproval. Then, bringing the anxiety to its next level, I became certain that he was right, that the anxiety I was feeling did spring from some deep-rooted prudery, a discomfort with anything but the most traditional displays of sexuality, and that this meant (moving on quickly to the next level now) that the anxiety I'd been struggling with ever since I lost my virginity wasn't so much a genetic problem or an emotional disorder as it was a kind of sex phobia, a conclusion that scared and disoriented me because it directly contradicted my image of myself as open-minded and progressive and suggested that perhaps at heart I was really conservative and rigid and hung up on all sorts of things I didn't know I was hung up on . . . and I became so entangled by all this, as Hjartarson talked with great energy about the different lengths, shapes, circumferences, and functionalities of the specimens available to the North Atlantic phallus collector, that I began to sweat right through my shirt.

Much more about sweat in a moment. First, a more abstract problem related to the social pressures of fact-checking. A checker doesn't just spend a lot of his time calling strangers, he spends a lot of his time calling strangers who happen to be internationally renowned experts in their fields. Moreover, these strangers happen to be internationally renowned experts in fields about which, more often than not, the checker hasn't even read an introductory textbook. This is inevitable. Unless you plan on getting up to speed

---

* In his article, Murphy notes that an elderly Icelandic farmer named Páll Arason had promised to donate his penis to the museum upon his demise. From what I can tell, Arason, who would now be in his late nineties, remains alive and attached to his member.

in, say, applied molecular physics in a couple of weeks, you're going to need to find and beg the help of a lot of trusted authorities. Fortunately, trusted authorities are generally very nice and generous people. One gets the sense that they enjoy trying to explain their disciplines to ordinary mortals. But the fact remains that they know everything and you know nothing, and this makes it not only intimidating to have a conversation but difficult even to come up with the vocabulary without which a productive conversation will be impossible. Far worse than mere discomfort and status anxiety, however, is how these interactions make it hard even to function in your work, because being internationally renowned experts who sometimes speak in incomprehensible jargon, these people have the habit of exposing the job you're being paid $30k plus benefits per annum to do as possibly completely bogus. They have this habit because they, and not you, are the ones who are qualified to judge the ultimate truth of the piece of writing you have called to discuss. What you are qualified to do is slash facts off a sheet of paper, one by one, until you've slashed them all. But as Meeker says, there's a big difference between confirming facts and establishing reality: "You can get every single detail right and it still won't mean the whole is true." This is why some of the most anxiety-provoking assignments a checker can get are the ones where the author and the expert are one and the same: It makes you feel fraudulent and useless to check the math of gods. It makes you ask yourself some unsettling questions about Truth. It makes you wonder if maybe you've hitched your wagon to the wrong epistemological horse. It makes you want to go back through your assignments and underline everything, every *and, the, if,* and *but*—or else nothing at all. It makes you wonder if you have the first inkling of what's good for you.

12.

the pits

Sweat: it is the great unspoken foe of the chronically anxious. It has no rival. Gnashed cuticles can be bandaged. Tears can be choked back. Intimations of catastrophe can be kept secret. But sweat—sweat is the mark of Cain.

Millennia ago, when Homo sapiens were evolving on the African plains, it was necessary to sweat when you sensed danger. Sweat cooled your body so you wouldn't overheat as you fled a predator. Sweat made your body slippery so you would be harder to grab hold of. Nature was wise to give us sweat glands. Then, in the 1920s, Freon was synthesized and nature's plan was forever altered. In the modern, climate-controlled office building, sweat has no practical use whatsoever. All it can do is expose a person's jitters to those around him, causing him to grow more jittery, causing him to sweat more, causing him to grow more jittery, causing him to sweat more, and so on and so forth in a soul-degrading circle of humiliation and dread. Among the most important questions a contemporary anxiety sufferer has to ask himself, therefore, is, "What should I do about my arm-pits?"

The web site livingwithanxiety.com gives the following advice regarding excessive sweating, a condition known in medical terms as hyperhidrosis: "A good way to prevent this is to relax, so you can control triggering stress that causes this anxiety symptom." This is somewhat less than helpful, like saying to a person in horrible pain because cancer is eating into his bones, "A good way to prevent this is not to allow your cells to proliferate, so you can control triggering tumors that cause this cancer symptom." The fact of the matter is, so long as a person remains anxious the only thing he will be able to do about his sweat, short of removing or paralyzing his sweat glands (some dermatologists offer Botox injections for hyperhidrosis), is conceal it.

Dark clothing is advisable. So is a jacket of some sort, though in warm weather it will exacerbate the problem and cause the cluelessly observant to inquire why you are overdressed. The most effective method I've found so far is to use a material of some sort to soak up the perspiration as it comes. You have to choose your material wisely, however. Once during a temp job I wedged a wad of toilet paper into my underarms to stanch the flow. This worked well until I was called over to consult with my supervisor. As I was leaning over her desk to explain a report I had written the wad dislodged, rolled down my shirt sleeve, and landed beside her keyboard with a sickening *splat*.

Sometime later, in a state of desperation, I discovered sweat pads. I had been assigned to write an article about American expatriates in Dubai, where the average temperature during my stay was going to be about 170 degrees in the shade. This ruled out a sports coat and sent me on a frenzied hunt for a product that would get me through the trip unmortified. It wasn't long before

I learned of a company called Kleinert's—"The World's Authority on Sweat Protection." The company's signature product is the disposable sweat pad, which it describes as "highly absorbent, noiseless, thin, discreet, convenient, easily applied disposable unisex underarm shields which adhere (peel & stick) securely to all fabrics including silks providing outstanding protection from odors and wet-thru staining." I ordered a case of twenty-four, enough to get both of my underarms through ten soggy days of reporting.

It fortified my confidence to read that the company has been manufacturing sweat pads since the Grant administration. Once I was in the desert, however, I was forced to conclude that in their nearly 140 years of business the good folks at Kleinert's had yet to encounter a case as acute as mine. By lunchtime on most days, the sweat had fully inundated the pads and begun to transcend their boundaries, producing a corona of moisture beneath each arm that was even more conspicuous than an old-fashioned, solid sweat stain. There was also an adhesion problem. Kleinert's is justly proud of its adhesive technology. The shields, which are shaped like morbidly obese butterflies, come outfitted with three parallel strips of tape that adhere wonderfully to your average male dress shirt—too wonderfully, was the problem. Perhaps the fault lay not with Kleinert's but with the piercing intensity of the Dubai heat, but on more than one occasion the glue from the tape seeped into the fabric of my shirts, resulting in permanent strips of darkened material that look, ironically, like sweat stains.

The experience soured me for a while on sweat pads. I took to wearing a lot of black, and stayed home as much as possible. Then, one average Sunday afternoon, my wife returned from Costco carrying a box of 96-count jumbo packs of Always Ultra Thin™ feminine hygiene pads with Flexi-Wings and LeakGuard Core™ barriers. ("This is gonna last me through menopause!"

she said), and I had one of those Archimedes-in-the-bathtub moments.

"Of course," I thought. "Why hadn't I thought of that before?" Naturally, the Kleinert's pads had been inadequate. How many people buy disposable underarm shields? Not a lot. But there are more than three billion women on the planet. Feminine hygiene is a $13 billion a year business. Thirteen billion dollars buys you a lot of high-class R&D. It buys you absorbency so cutting edge it's like the sweat is being sucked into a different dimension. It buys you adhesiveness that's like some alien technology; you can peel the pad off your shirt and put it back on again a dozen times and it'll stay just as sticky as before. It buys you maximum performance with minimum size, discomfort, or audible rustling.

From then on, whenever I have had to leave the house to meet someone it behooves me not to repulse, I have worn beneath my arms a product expertly designed by a multinational corporation to absorb eighty milliliters of menstrual blood at a wearing.

I wish I had known thirteen years ago what I know now about the versatility of the maxi pad, for it was my sweating that began to make life at *The Atlantic* truly intolerable. A painful pattern to my existence emerged. Every night I would go home to rejuvenate myself with drink and sleep, and every morning I would return to confront a series of forces that substantiated and anatomized the very anxiety I was desperate to escape: the galley pages color-coded like the old federal terror alert system; clippings, reference material, and transcripts testifying to the delusion that, with the correct titration of effort, solid ground could be found; the imposing editorial staff watching over my shoulder to make sure that even the assertions made in the poetry were sufficiently verified.

By 10 a.m. my undershirt would be drenched. By 10:30 the sweat would breach the outer garment, planting a seed of moisture at the bulge beneath the arm where the two seams of fabric intersect. By 11 a.m. the seed would sprout, creeping up to the shoulder from both sides, down the trunk, and down the arm. Then it would become all about flood control. For the rest of the day I would make frequent trips to the men's room to get myself dry.

The men's room at *The Atlantic* didn't have an electric dryer. All it had was a canister of thin paper towels stamped with dots and folded into thirds. I made these towels work for me as best I could. I would take a stack with me into the handicapped stall, remove my shirt, line my hand with a towel or two, and squeeze first one shirt underarm and then another in my fist, to sop up the worst of it. Then I'd start scrubbing. The trick was to scrub very fast. The faster I scrubbed the more friction and heat was produced. But I had to be careful not to scrub so fast that it would compromise the structural integrity of the paper towel, which had the habit of disintegrating when it took on too much water and which, in the process of disintegrating, deposited dozens of white pellets on the insides of my shirts. (They looked like miniature cotton fields.) All this cut down markedly on the life span of my dress shirts, but it did the trick—for a while. An hour or so later I would be back on my way to the bathroom, arms pinned to my sides like Frankenstein's monster.

I tried not to consider what my coworkers thought was wrong with me. Dysentery? Urinary-tract infection? Bulimia? All I knew was that it was a deeply unproductive and disagreeable way to spend my days. On my trips to the men's room I would pass the office of Peter Davison, the longtime poetry editor. Davison had been a protégé of Robert Frost's, a friend of Robert Lowell's, and a lover of Sylvia Plath's. I would much rather have been sitting with Davison hearing stories about dead poets than ministering to my armpits. I'd much rather have been getting my eyelashes weed-whacked than ministering to my armpits. As in college, it was the lack of solitude that most rankled. Surrounded by people—and, of course, by my facts, my inextinguishable facts—I felt as if I were living in an emergency room, with all the light-headed un-reality that setting causes.

Yet I also felt, for the first time, truly and sincerely pissed. It was enough already. Enough! I'd reached that point that comes in the life of most anxiety sufferers when, fed up by the constant waking torture, dejected and buckled but not yet crushed, they at last turn to their anxiety, to themselves, and say, "Listen here: Fuck you. Fuck you! I am sick and fucking tired of this bullshit. I refuse to let you win. I am not going to take it anymore. You are ruining my fucking life and you MUST FUCKING DIE!"

Unfortunately, this approach rarely solves the problem. Anxiety doesn't bend to absolutism. You have to take a subtler, more reasoned approach. But that doesn't mean anger is totally unhelpful. Being pissed off is a strong cocktail for the will. It stiffens the spine. It strengthens resolve. It makes a person less willing to run away from the anxiety and more willing to walk into it, which you're going to have to do, ultimately, if you don't want to end up a complete agoraphobic. Anger breeds defiance, and defiance is inspiriting. It's good to refuse to give in to anxiety. You just have to know how much you can take.

I have on my desk a summons from the Supreme Court of the State of New York, County of New York, stamped by the county clerk's office October 1, 2003. The summons is stapled to a sixteen-page complaint suing me and the publishing house Houghton Mifflin for libel for $23 million. When I received the complaint I was living in a roach-infested former tenement building in Manhattan. The lawsuit was the culmination of an ordeal that had begun almost three years earlier with the publication of my first piece of writing—a long, in-depth article about electroshock therapy. The article, which was titled "Shock and Disbelief," was a professional triumph for me. It appeared in *The Atlantic* when I was twenty-three and was selected to be included in Houghton Mifflin's *Best American Science and Nature Writing* anthology. It was also a personal disaster. The article resulted, in order of occurrence, in the following: the longest, most debilitating bout with anxiety of my life thus far; my panic-stricken, half-crazed self-removal from the staff of *The Atlantic*; the termination of a two-year-long cohabiting relationship with a beautiful and intelligent woman; grief and despair of Old Testament proportions; and an extended period of psychic bottom-dwelling.

In retrospect, it should have been clear from the start that electroshock therapy was not the wisest subject with which to pop my journalistic cherry. In mental health circles, electroshock is as controversial as partial-birth abortion is in political circles. The controversy breaks down along fairly clear lines. Psychiatrists are generally in favor of electroshock. They have seen the treatment pull people out of profound, catatonic depressions, and back from the cusp of suicide. In *Shock Therapy: A History of Electroconvulsive Treatment in Mental Illness*, the psychiatrist David Healy and the historian Edward Shorter call electroshock "powerful and beneficial . . . safe and effective." They write: "ECT is, in a sense, the penicillin of psychiatry."

Those who oppose the procedure have seen it ruin lives, often their own. They argue that electroshock can have calamitous effects on cognition, personality, and especially memory, and that it is no more legitimate a medical treatment than knocking someone over the head with a cinderblock. In *Doctors of Deception: What They Don't Want You to Know About Shock Treatment,* Linda Andre, a writer and activist who underwent a course of electroshock in the early 1980s—and the plaintiff in the complaint against me*—writes:

> The memory "loss" that happens with shock treatment is really memory erasure. A period of time is wiped out as if it never happened. Unlike memory loss associated with other conditions such as Alzheimer's, which come on gradually and allow patients and families to anticipate and prepare for the loss to some extent, the amnesia associated with electroconvulsive therapy . . . is sudden, violent, and unexpected. Your life is essentially unlived.

Electroshock therapy is the sort of topic that makes the salivary glands of your typical magazine editor work double-time. In addition to the built-in conflict, it has a colorful history (the procedure was developed, in Italy in the 1930s, by applying electrodes to the anuses, mouths, and heads of stray dogs), a counterintuitive slant (what sounds brutal and primitive may in fact be therapeutic and empirically validated), madness, science, even a whiff of celebrity: Ernest Hemingway, Judy Garland, and Lou Reed all underwent shock therapy. (Reed had shock therapy when he was a teenager; his parents were trying to rid him of homosexual urges.) It is a topic rich with all kinds of complexities—medical, statistical, ethical, legal, narrative—and so one ideally covered by a journalist who knows what he's doing.

I was not that journalist. I was not a journalist at all. I had never reported before, not even for my high school paper. I had never

---

* See pages 227–30 of Andre's book for a seriously unflattering portrayal of yours truly.

physically held, let alone read the articles in, a psychiatric journal. The only person I had ever interviewed was an electrician (coincidentally), and that was for a report I wrote in the third grade. At the time I proposed the article the only qualification I could claim was my work as a fact-checker. Checking had at least introduced me to the skills a good journalist needs: the ability to navigate the byways of databases and archives, to mine expertise for resonant generalizations, to sniff down elusive details and sources. But a journalist needs to know how to do so much more than that. He needs to be able to accumulate and digest innumerable discrete bits of information, many of them contradictory, and weave the most pertinent and telling bits into a text of a preordained length that honors both the letter and the spirit of the subject, satisfies the biases and pet curiosities of the editors on whose good dispositions the publication of the article depends, and holds the attention of thousands of anonymous readers with very little time or brain space to waste on something that isn't super-interesting or -essential.

I had none of these skills. But I had watched the powers-that-be at *The Atlantic* hold the clammy hands of enough neophytes and incompetents—had watched with amazement as, time and again, they took an inferior piece of writing and alchemized it into something resembling literature—not to be paralyzed by the task ahead of me. "Not to be paralyzed" is indeed an understatement. I was soothed. If in the case of my mother I resented my anxious tendency to negate my will in favor of someone else's, in the case of *The Atlantic* I invited it. It felt comforting to place myself in the hands of someone else's competence, to feel that there was something authoritative and institutional backing me up, nudging me in the right direction, promising to save me. Giving over your will, I was learning, could be a balm as well as an acid.

William James knew this well and said it best. In *The Varieties of Religious Experience,* he describes the many ways that the "sick soul" can be redeemed: "[The] new birth may be away from religion into incredulity; or it may be from moral scrupulosity into freedom and license; or it may be produced by the irruption into the individual's life of some stimulus or passion, such as love, ambition, cupidity, revenge, or patriotic devotion."

As it happened, love was irrupting into my life at just this time, too. On a trip to New York to attend a party thrown by my brother Scott and his new wife, I met a girl, and the immediate and mutual attraction between us went a long way toward quieting my mind. It redirected my attention from myself to someone else, from my hatred of my nature to my affection for someone else's, from despair and demoralization to excitement and anticipation. Of course, feeling soothed by love turned out to be as temporary and full of folly as feeling soothed by authority turned out to be. You can't be converted out of anxiety any more than you can be shocked out of being gay. No one can do the work but yourself.

But both were nice while they lasted.

In a way it was like being an anti-checker, those long months of nights, weekends, vacations, and lunch hours I spent reporting and writing the article. During my salaried hours: stonewalling authors, uncited claims, unreturned calls, slogs through soporific government reports and hernia-inducing tomes on subjects in which I had no interest. During my catch-as-catch-can hours: information gathered steadily and by choice, no fear of error because there was no imminent deadline and because there were safety nets in place—and because error was no longer the point. Knowledge was. For once I wasn't inspecting; I was building.

But there was a blind spot to my work: I was afraid of madness. I was terrified by the very thought of it. I was terrified of being contaminated by it. This isn't unusual. Physical disease and mental illness are the two most common fears known to humankind. For the anxious, in whom the fears are naturally pronounced, it seems to be a matter of disposition which will be dominant. The best litmus test is a panic attack, during which some will be convinced they are dying and others that they are going insane. I thought I'd go insane. When I wasn't in a panic, I simply felt a revulsion to anything that smacked of madness.

Over the years, therapists have tried to disavow me of my fear of insanity in much the way that another web site devoted to anxiety tries to disavow its readers of the fear. "No one with panic attacks and anxiety has ever gone 'crazy,' " the site claims. "In fact, because you realize that you have panic attacks, this is just another indication that you are *not* going crazy. People that 'go crazy' lose contact with reality. Anxious people are *too much in contact* with reality. Thus, people with panic and anxiety problems NEVER 'go crazy.' It simply cannot happen."

Counsel like this has never worked on me; you can't reassure someone out of an atavistic fear. The only thing that has helped, perversely, is devoting a decade of my life to writing about mental illness—exposing myself to insanity until the urge to recoil is brought to bay. I have watched a man so tormented by compulsions that he actually applied to have two lesions surgically burned into his brain in a last-ditch effort for relief. I have sat in the back of a sweltering auditorium as dozens of people discussed the disembodied voices they walk around listening to. I have interviewed the schizophrenic, the schizoaffective, the depressive, and the manic-depressive, and I have pored over accounts of mental disintegration from Nebuchadnezzar to Zelda Fitzgerald.

I have done all this, in large part, because I suspect my fear of madness improperly influenced my electroshock article, and I have wanted to correct for the error. In reporting, I looked at both sides of the issue. I used *The Atlantic*'s clout to schedule interviews with everyone who seemed important in the debate about the politics and science of electroshock. I got in touch with Linda Andre, director of the Committee for Truth in Psychiatry, an organization made up of several hundred former electroshock patients, and interviewed her at an Italian restaurant on the Upper West Side. She brought her son, who quietly did his homework while Andre outlined the deceptions and venality of the psychiatric establishment. In a sun-drenched dining room in an exquisite Long Island house I interviewed Max Fink, a voluminous, aging psychiatrist who has studied and promoted electroshock for more than fifty years. I interviewed a representative of the Citizens Commission on Human Rights, a lobbying organization affiliated with the Church of Scientology that has been active in trying to get electroshock restricted in several states. I interviewed clinicians who presented electroshock as an invaluable treatment with an unfortunate history of abuse and a range of possible side effects. I interviewed Roland Kohloff, the principal timpanist for the New York Philharmonic, who credited electroshock with saving his life. And, on a cool fall day in 2000, I drove out to McLean Hospital, the legendary facility where Lowell, Plath, and Anne Sexton had all been treated, and I watched as doctors administered electroshock to a desperate-looking middle-aged man in tennis shoes and a purple shirt. They fastened a blood-pressure cuff around his ankle and injected him with a muscle relaxant. During the procedure, only his foot twitched.

Given the entrenchment of the opposing sides—the activists disdainful of the integrity of the psychiatrists, the psychiatrists resentful of the severe rhetoric of the activists—the article I wrote over the next few months was bound to elicit criticism. The article gave ample space to electroshock's detractors, delineating their backgrounds and presenting their complaints at great length—but it failed to treat those complaints with seriousness or compassion. It lent credence to the view that electroshock can sometimes cause profound memory loss—but it made no real effort to explore the medical science behind that side effect, to describe its emotional costs, or (most egregious from the point of view of electroshock's critics) to investigate the claim that in many cases patients are still administered electroshock without informed consent. The article couldn't do any of those things—*I* couldn't do any of those things—because to do them would have meant inserting myself into the experiences of people whose lives were defined, rightly or wrongly, by madness. It would have meant having to empathize with some truly horrifying feelings of anger, betrayal, and trauma, and I simply couldn't do that. My anxiety wouldn't even let me get close to that fire, for fear of falling in. And so I came down, ultimately, on the side of order—of a refined medical treatment meted out cautiously, meticulously, undramatically, and usually successfully, with the comforting sanction of esteemed professional organizations. I came down in favor of electroshock.

When the article was published it was lauded by almost every one of the mental health professionals who chose to comment. Almost. Fink wrote me an e-mail that seemed to suggest that by giving voice to electroshock's detractors my article would dissuade seriously ill patients from seeking out or assenting to the treatment and would thereby result in the deaths by suicide of thousands. I had blood on my young hands. The other side of the line was more crowded with dissent. On *The Atlantic*'s online comments page, I was pilloried for incompetence. In the lawsuit

Andre eventually filed, she counted that the comments were 70–2 against the article, and offered some choice denunciations:

'This article feels like marketing; it saddens me to see *Atlantic's* reporting so biased.' (Comment #4) 'Journalistic standards that would apply to high school newspapers are thrown out the window when it comes to electroshock.' (Comment #10) 'DANIEL SMITH IS NO JOURNALIST.' (Comment #12) 'In Journalism 101, we were taught the basics, and I'm afraid that Mr. Smith has ignored what he should have learned in college . . . Daniel, you should have CHECKED your piece.' (Comment #15)

One commenter went through the article line by line, pointing out all the inaccuracies in a document that ran for many single-spaced pages. He fact-checked my article! I got several calls from Andre, demanding answers. The editors heard from Andre, demanding answers. The journalist Liz Spikol, later a prominent blogger on mental health issues, responded with a column titled "Shocked and Appalled." The last line of her piece was, "I'm thinking maybe it's time for Daniel Smith, the author of 'Shock and Disbelief,' to have his head examined."

My sentiments exactly. By then I was well on my way to a mindset that made my response to losing my virginity seem like a pleasant afternoon nap. I still had to work. I still had to sift through other people's articles for errors. I still had to monitor my underarms for moisture. And now I had to contend as well with the mounting indictments of my own potential errors and the consequences I was being told they would have—not on me, which was self-evident, but on other people, and on the world.

Consequences. It is not a favored concept for the anxious. During those times when I am berating myself for all that I've done wrong, all the mistakes I believe I've made, I call Scott and he reminds me that the only choices that have permanent consequences are creating life and ending it. I hadn't killed anyone or knocked anyone up. I hadn't even acted maliciously. I had worked hard and tried my best and hoped to do well, to do good. But the thought I could not shake was that there was no way to know what effect those 500,000 or so copies of the magazine circulating out there in the world were going to have, whether they would coax some unlucky person in distress to have electroshock and thereby have his memory erased, or whether they would coax someone in distress not to have electroshock and thereby to sink further into distress and self-destruction. The deed was done, and the result could be anything.

And for what? Toward what end? A *byline?* For that I'd opened myself up to scorn, demands for a retraction, legal threats? I wasn't Christopher Hitchens. I took no pleasure in controversy. I was a junior editor twenty months out of college. All I'd wanted was to write and be published. A little light literary glory, that was all. Instead I'd called up a storm. A great tidal swell of panic overtook me and refused to recede. No permanence save life or death? Tell that to my brain, big brother. It didn't hear the news. It was too busy counting bodies. Every day at work the postmortem continued, every day I was reassured by my superiors that all was well— this was journalism, this was how it sometimes went—and every day I became less able to hear a positive or logical word anyone said. The sensation was like when your ears fill with fluid and you can't get them to drain: a cocoon of the self. I stumbled viscously through. I began to dream of being mad and institutionalized, face up on a gurney, electrodes at my slick temples. Nooses. Pill bottles. Pistols. Bridges. Knives. The absence of choice. The absence of consequence. If this was life, what was the point?

13.

anxious love

Dear Dan,

You are sitting now in the Duomo—a Tintoretto here, a Pisano there, Jesus everywhere—and you are feeling down. What it is is something you've felt before when it seems as if life has placed you in a position in which you do not want to be. No, let's clarify: You have put yourself in a position in which you do not want to be. You are feeling (we're going to have to use that tapioca word quite a bit, I'm afraid) what you have learned to call "anxious," a term it's a little hard to define but that can include a number of psychopathological elements: fear, dread, self-loathing, homesickness, a desire to retreat into some place where the self-reflection can be total and you can luxuriate in self-abasement for hours (bed, e.g.), a tendency toward questioning your decisions both on the micro and macro scales (this one maybe should be moved to the top of the list) . . . let's see, what else? Ah yes: physical symptoms. These may include loss of appetite (in Tuscany! Sweet Moses!), nausea, a lump in the throat, lack of short-/long-term memory, lethargy, the icicle of course. No decreased libido. After all, you're twenty-three yrs. old.

There's got to be more . . . did I mention self-loathing? Yes? Did I really put enough emphasis on taking every big and little decision and scrutinizing it as if it were literally a matter of life or death? I did? Well, then, how about the insatiable (because who would do it?) urge to call your mother and cry?

Now, if all this is a disease, as I've been told, what is the cure? <u>Is</u> there a cure? No, probably there isn't. But there is a course of action. On the tortured decisions and catastrophizing and dwelling, always remember the following: IT IS MORE THAN LIKELY THAT THIS WILL <u>NOT</u> KILL YOU. Also: DANIEL, YOU MUST GIVE YOURSELF A BREAK. THIS IS NOT EASY. IT IS NOT FUN. BUT IT CAN BE IF YOU RE-PEAT AFTER ME: IT'S JUST LIFE. IT IS NOT PERFECT. THERE ARE NO ASSURANCES. NOT EVERYONE WILL LIKE YOU. NOT EVERYTHING YOU HAVE TO DO WILL BE ENJOYABLE.

Larger now:

YOU ARE HUMAN!
YOU ARE FALLIBLE!
YOU WILL ENJOY LIFE MUCH MORE IF YOU ACCEPT—NO, <u>EMBRACE</u>—THE FACT THAT THERE IS NO SUCH THING AS A GOOD DECISION AND A BAD DE-CISION.
THERE ARE ONLY <u>DECISIONS</u>.
MAKE THEM, FUCK UP, ENJOY, RE-PEAT.

This passage was written in the central cathedral in Lucca, in northern Tuscany—the Cattedrale di San Martino, named after Martin of Tours, the first saint to have the dubious honor of having to endure his biblically allotted threescore and ten rather than being burned, beheaded, stoned, crucified, or tortured to death in his prime. In the marble composition notebook in which it appears the passage bears the title, "Painfully Obvious Letter to Myself." It isn't dated, but I know it was written in April 2001, in the middle of a two-week trip to Rome, Florence, Lucca, Siena, and Venice I took with my then live-in girlfriend, Joanna. That, it rattles the mind now to realize, is the undesirable "position" to which the passage refers, the event of which it moans, "IT IS NOT FUN": a luxurious Italian tour with a lovely young woman, filled with food, wine, art, and lovemaking.

The trip took place two months after the publication of my electroshock article and twenty months after Joanna and I met, and was expected to further cement the relationship we had both believed was progressing steadily toward marriage. Instead it harnessed and distilled the years of mounting anxiety that preceded it and showed Joanna that the young man she'd fallen for was far too caught up in himself, too nervous, confused, and deluded— too selfish—to love anyone, and therefore to be loved in return. By the end of the year, she'd broken up with me. It would be years before I would win her back. In the interim I would have to learn how to wall my anxiety off from others, to seal it up inside myself so securely that its indiscriminate uncertainty would no longer be able to influence or infect the people I loved—which is to say, my *feelings* for the people I loved. I would have to learn how to protect love itself from anxiety.

●　●　●

For the anxious, love—the most redemptive of experiences and the pinnacle of human relations—is a hell of agonizing indecision, corrupted joys, unreliable desires, unbearable self-realizations, and the most intense, paradoxical loneliness. And guilt. Above all, guilt—implacable and vicious. Because in love an anxious person becomes a persecutor as well as a masochist. He doesn't intend to hurt anyone, least of all his beloved. He isn't a sadist. But he is toxic, and merely by yielding to his affection he draws an innocent into the zone of pollution. Psychological self-abuse becomes psychological assault. In love, anxiety takes victims.

When I met Joanna, in the summer of 1999—freshly graduated, freshly employed, paralytically anxious—I didn't know any of this. I had been in love just once before and it had been unrequited. I had never had a girlfriend, I had never had a long-term sexual partner. I had never had the chance to see how my anxiety performed in the romantic field. I had never given myself the chance. All through high school and college the same comedy repeated itself over and over again: Boy meets girl, girl likes boy, girl expresses like for boy, boy agonizes day and night over the potential consequences of girl's like for boy, ultimately convincing himself that the end result of a single date to the movies will be an inextricable entanglement, a loveless marriage, a crippling divorce, and years of shame, penury, and clinical depression. Boy has friend tell girl that boy has contracted double pneumonia and will be unavailable for six to eight weeks.

Joanna's charm and misfortune was to be the first person to break this cycle. What possessed her to get close enough even to be implicated in this milestone is a mystery. I've studied photographs of myself from the party where we met and can detect not a hint of allure in the spectral young man staring back at me. I look like I'm on a weekend pass from a methadone clinic.

The haphazard beard on my cheeks is at once sinister and faintly rabbinical. My skin has an insomniac pallor, there are charcoal-colored circles beneath my eyes, and I am wearing rumpled, out-of-style clothes. It seems more likely that I'd attract a case of head lice than a woman.

Yet there was Joanna: bronze-skinned, bright-eyed, full-lipped, with a modest glittering diamond in each ear. I caught her looking at me as I loitered by my brother's bookshelves, trying to seem as absorbed as possible by a paperback copy of Kant's *Prolegomena to Any Future Metaphysics*—to ward off humans. I thought maybe I had guacamole on my chinos. Then my sister-in-law led Joanna over and introduced her as a coworker—they had adjacent cubicles at a midtown nonprofit, where they were paid to distribute a billionaire's money—and I had to work quickly to process three very unlikely deductions. First, despite my unsightliness and her beauty, Joanna appeared to have been neither coerced nor threatened into speaking with me. Second, despite the sharp panic lodged in my neck, chest, gut, and groin, Joanna appeared either not to notice or not to care. Third, despite all established precedent, Joanna's presence was not only not exacerbating my anxiety, it seemed actually to be tamping it down. I noticed this immediately. She was like a living, talking Xanax tablet. Just the sight of her—sipping from a plastic cup of wine, nodding at my answers to her questions, idly uncurling a strand of her hair—was a tonic. The effect was so unfamiliar it was almost distracting. For the rest of the party we were inseparable, and as we chatted in a hallway, or joked flirtatiously, or ate food off each other's plates, I kept having to will myself not to think, *I am chatting in a hallway with a woman, I am joking flirtatiously with a woman, I am eating food off a woman's plate. I am engaging in an exchange that the arbiters of social behavior deem a sign of virility and health.*

It may have been that I'd internalized the fundamental safety of the situation: a pre-vetted woman in a familial setting I'd be leaving in fewer than twenty-four hours for a city two states away. But even the internalization of safety, rather than the internalization of hazard, contingency, and flux, would have been something to note in my diary, and as I drove along I-95 the next morning, Boston-bound, a mountain of fact-checking documents awaiting my attention, not even the tractor-trailers bearing murderously down on my car could uproot the new confidence I felt the encounter had planted within me.

I expected nothing to come of it. At Joanna's request we had exchanged numbers, but I'd assumed she was just capping off the flirtation. "The next time you're in town look me up," and so on. But the very next night the phone rang at my bedside and there she was again, soft and nervous, reintroducing herself unnecessarily.

I was delighted to discover that the therapeutic sorcery Joanna had worked on me at the party worked long distance, too. Listening to her talk about her life in New York—about her work at the foundation, about her passion for public education, about her friends and roommates—I detected a bizarre clarity materializing in my mind, an unfamiliar ability to differentiate between fear and excitement. These sensations had always been frustratingly similar, starting as they do with the same adrenaline flush, causing the same bodily disorientation. But I felt no confusion about what the chill in my chest and the tingling in my limbs now signified. This wasn't fear. This was elation.

The rest happened with an inevitability that makes it hard to account for. We spoke for more than two hours that night, we spoke for more than two hours the next night, and we spoke for more than two hours every night after that. During the days I focused on the articles the editors assigned me, and during the nights I focused on the woman who had assigned herself to me. After three weeks, I couldn't stand it anymore and laid down my credit card for a flight to New York. From that point on, we went back and forth every other weekend. After nine months, I couldn't stand that either and asked my roommate to move out and Joanna to move in. Let my sister-in-law give the billionaire's money away alone for a while. Joanna was my salvation. She was needed up north.

Poor lovers of the anxious! Poor martyrs! Poor Joanna! In moving in with me she could not possibly have known what she was getting herself into. I hinted at my anxiety here and there, but when I did it was with the self-deprecating ethnic pride I'd picked up from Roth—that clowning Jewish swagger—rather than with the full historical, clinical, and necessary truth. Joanna should have been informed of my anxiety the same way prospective pet owners are informed of a dog's distemper.

But, then, what incentive was there to tell the truth? Not only did I not want to drive Joanna away, but in her presence I couldn't see the truth. The truth she needed to know was, so far as I was concerned, the old truth, the pre-Joanna truth. With her in my life there was no old truth. There was only the wonderful new Joanna truth: stability, sensuality, other-centeredness, affection. An optimistic psychological future. I had a few apprehensions about undergoing so significant a change, but I chalked them up to just that: apprehensions about undergoing a significant change. Perfectly normal to feel those. Nothing pathological about it.

Those who knew me better than I knew myself had an easier time seeing the peril in the scenario. "Are you sure?" asked a college friend. "You're moving pretty quickly with this chick." "Joanna's great," said Scott. "I love Joanna. She's like family already. But think this over some more, buddy. *Consider* it. You've never even had a girlfriend before." "What's the big rush?" said my mother. "Why not keep things the way they are for a little while? At least you can get separate apartments the first year. I'll help you look!" My friend Kate later claimed that when I told her Joanna was moving in with me, she saw a flash of panic in my eyes.

Probably she did see a flash of panic. The germ was certainly there. But it was veiled, obscured beneath the large, noisy, delicious distraction of my passion for Joanna. No, Joanna could not have known the difficulties that were coming. I, having never been in love before, could not have known the difficulties that were coming. But they came. Joanna moved to Boston in the summer of 2000. Six months later, when my electroshock article was published and a fresh gust of anxiety toppled me, Joanna was toppled, too.

The problem wasn't that the germ of anxiety inside me grew and strangled my love. That would have been relatively simple. With a certifiably dead love I might have been able to say, to everyone's benefit, "Sorry. I made a mistake. I shouldn't have asked you here. Now let's go see if we can get your old job back!" The problem was that my anxiety colonized my love. Anxiety is, among other things, a disorder of choice. It begins with a doubt about the self and if that doubt is not isolated and slaughtered immediately it will breed like vermin. The doubt will populate every precinct of the mind, no matter how sacred.

At first Joanna wasn't implicated in my anxiety about my article. I brooded plenty about my reportorial and potentially moral failings. I brooded about the slipperiness of truth, the double-edged nature of success, and the ethical conundra at the heart of the journalist-subject relationship. I spent hours hashing over the details of other journalistic controversies, in particular the one Roth mentioned in his letter to Whitworth: the psychoanalyst Jeffrey Masson's libel suit against the writer Janet Malcolm. I rushed out and bought Malcolm's *The Journalist and the Murderer,* and was both comforted and appalled by its notorious opening claim that "Every journalist who is not too stupid or too full of himself to notice what is going on knows that what he does is morally indefensible." But I kept Joanna out of it. I needed Joanna. She was my cheerleader and my confidante. She was the person I came home to each night with my Willy Loman look, fatigued and demoralized by the strain of remaining conscious for more than eight hours at a stretch. She was the one who poured me drinks, stroked my back, and said, "Things will get better soon. I promise. You just have to let this blow over."

It blew over. After a few weeks, the online comments trickled off, the letter writers moved on to other alleged abhorrences, and the editors appeared satisfied that no legal or reputational harm would come to them or me. Yet promise or no, things didn't get better. The stimulus disappeared but the response remained, and so, like a hermit crab stripped of its shell, my anxiety went looking for another home and found one in the woman who was sharing mine. A terrible pattern began, an abusive dance in four recurring steps.

Step One: mounting uncertainty. Perhaps what I'd felt for Joanna all along, I began to say to myself, was not love but infatuation or desire or desperation or lust. Maybe it was a weak man's need for emotional shelter. Maybe it was a temporary masking of loneliness. Maybe it was what Roth said at the start of *The Anatomy Lesson*: "When he is sick, every man wants his mother; if she's not around, other women must do." Whatever the case, it had been sheer naïveté, a folly bordering on self-destruction, to have Joanna move in with me. I was now more trapped in proximity than ever before.

Step Two: withdrawal. Increasingly doubtful of my affection, as well as embarrassed by my anxiety and resentful of Joanna's inability to calm it, I'd become sullen, neglectful, and blatantly discontented. In short: an asshole. I would put Joanna down, dismiss her ideas, ignore her requests, and in general make it clear in a thousand unsubtle ways that her presence in Boston, my apartment, and my life had become an awful burden to me.

Step Three: blowback. Registering my behavior, Joanna would respond with sadness and the fear that she had uprooted her life for someone who not only didn't love her but didn't even seem to like or respect her very much. Recriminations would follow. Tears. Slammed doors. Fertile silences. Stock scenes from the disintegration of every romance in the history of the world.

Step Four: retreat. Horrified by my cruelty, suddenly terrified by the prospect of life alone, I would dedicate myself to repairing the damage. Gourmet meals. Gerbera daisies. Amateur poetry. Proclamations of undying adoration. Anything and everything to win Joanna back to my side.

Push, pull. Push, pull. Push, pull. It was textbook battered woman syndrome, just without the beatings, and it placed me in illustrious company. Kierkegaard so badly tortured his beloved with his neurotic indecision that she fell into a depression; for eleven months he wavered maniacally between affection and aversion, devotion and abandonment. "So after all," she said when they'd finally broken off, "you have also played a terrible game with me." William James, who was beset by acute anxiety throughout his twenties and early thirties, afflicted his future wife with the same inconstancy; he wrote long, tormented letters in which he assiduously courted her and fended her off in the same short paragraphs. And then there is Kafka—the worst lover in the Western canon. For five years, Kafka strung his girlfriend and fiancée along, dedicating all the literary, intellectual, and polemical skills at his disposal to two contradictory goals: winning and keeping her hand, and proving to her that he was a "sick, weak, unsociable, taciturn, gloomy, stiff, almost helpless man" with whom life would be a complete disaster.

Joanna and I had been planning our trip to Italy almost as long as we had been living together. We studied *Lonely Planet,* we bought and listened to the Pimsleur tapes, we accumulated restaurant and *pensione* recommendations. The emphasis was to be on decadence and plain, unmitigated fun. But as the weeks and my anxiety progressed I began to attach a sense of immense obligation to the trip. If I was going to slip the binds of my neurosis and end the agonizing back-and-forth into which I'd forced us, I was going to need an ocean to help me. The geography of work and home was too constricting and familiar for a rebirth. And a rebirth was what I, and I and Joanna, needed.

That we were unlikely to get one I sensed even on the flight over. As Joanna flipped through the thick folder of travel articles, maps, and reviews she'd put together, I nursed an eight-dollar Budweiser and wondered whether a panic attack might compel the pilot to turn the plane around, and if so how he would announce this over the intercom. It'd have to be a real doozy of an attack, but I thought myself capable. It seemed my last chance to avoid what, I realized somewhere east of Newfoundland, was bound to be a catastrophic two weeks. Two weeks in a strange country! Two weeks of being perpetually side by side with another human being! Two weeks during which the need to appear chipper was going to be exponentially more oppressive than it had been at home.

For a while I managed to stifle myself. Except for a few fleeting, cherished exceptions—sharing a cigarette on the Ponte Sant' Angelo; napping together with the shutters open, tickled by the breeze; sunbathing in Siena's Piazza del Campo—I couldn't enjoy things, so it seemed only fair that I focus on concealing my unenjoyment. We'd each tapped our savings for the vacation. This way Joanna would at least get her money's worth.

It was a well-intentioned scheme, but it had two very large flaws. First, Joanna happens not to be an idiot. She can tell the difference between pleasure and suppressed panic. In addition to piquing her annoyance for being joyless, therefore, I was also piquing her annoyance for withholding my true feelings—a double crime. Second, the more stifling I did the more alienated from the world I became, and the more alienated from the world I became, the more I cleaved to the guilty content and madman logic of my anxiety. By the time we made it to Florence, about halfway through the trip, I was beginning to feel like a cross between the guy in *The Diving Bell and the Butterfly* and Raskolnikov—thoroughly locked-in to the most unstable of minds. All the lovely and luxurious things we did, all the picnics we had and masterpieces we saw and love we made, were wasted on me. I wasn't even there. I was back in Boston, staring at my article, obsessed by the harm I had purportedly done. *Convinced* of the harm I had purportedly done. Imagine: Lounging with my loving, devoted girlfriend in the Boboli Gardens on a warm spring day, all I could concentrate on was the application of 50 to 225 millicoulombs of electricity to the temporal lobes of catatonically depressed inpatients.

In Venice, in a *pensione* overlooking the Grand Canal, Joanna finally reached her limit. We had just set down our bags, I sighed one of the long, sorrow-of-the-cosmos sighs that were becoming my trademark, and Joanna turned on her heels and said, "You know, I can't remember the last time you told me you loved me." Here is where I tried out a theory I had been working up for just such an occasion. The theory was that if I were to stay as motionless and silent as possible—like a lizard trying to outwit a predator—Joanna would forget whatever she was demanding of me and carry on as before.

The theory failed.

"Well. Say something."

I stammered, then finally got it out: "I don't think I do love you anymore."

It was true, in its way, though it sounded awful out there in the world like that, audible and alive. Sometimes I loved Joanna. When I felt good, or very, very sleepy, or when we were in bed together, or when I'd had a milligram or more of Xanax. But increasingly I couldn't even see her anymore other than as an obstacle to the total self-enclosure toward which I was inclined. And how could you love someone if you can't even see them? Though if you can't see them why does it at the same time feel crucial that you keep them? And is the very idea of "keeping" someone a consequence of not being able to see them?

I was just starting to parse all this when, in my peripheral vision, I saw the first object soaring at me from across the room.

14.

brian

It took Joanna eight whole months to cut me loose. She was hurt and often confused, but she seemed to understand that the pain I was inflicting on her wasn't advertent but merely a spilling over of my own pain. She was no stranger to anxiety herself. She knew a bit about what it meant and what it felt like. And she loved me, the poor thing. She wanted to think the best. That summer, I proposed we find separate apartments; she agreed that a little distance might improve matters. That fall, I decided to resign from *The Atlantic*; she believed me when I said I was leaving to concentrate on writing. In truth, I quit because I couldn't bear being around people anymore.

The deciding indignity for Joanna was when I showed up at a holiday party at her new apartment two hours late, slurringly drunk, with a married friend who proceeded to pull off his wedding band and proposition one of the guests. (Me, years later: "I don't know how you lasted as long as you did." Joanna: "Low self-esteem.") Dumping me, she seemed gleeful and relieved, as if she'd just learned that a chronic disease she'd endured for years was at last in remission. I felt much the same way. I had been waiting for her to muster the courage I lacked. At last I wouldn't have to worry about hurting her anymore, or berate myself for being unable to stop.

The good feeling lasted forty-eight hours. Then I took to bed with a pinching headache and found that I couldn't get back up. For a full week I lay on my mattress on the floor, hemmed in by spent tissue boxes and pill canisters, snotty and stricken and fixated day and night on the hulking character flaws that had led me to sabotage the one true relationship I'd ever had and probably ever would. It was the old *Macbeth* feeling again, that self-referential psychosis. I couldn't do, see, hear, or smell anything without being reminded of what I'd demolished—without being reminded of Joanna. I couldn't watch movies. I couldn't read books. I couldn't watch TV. I couldn't read magazines. I couldn't even stare out the window: The trees, swaying, swayed like her. The birds were too exultant; it was like they were chirping to mock me. Even the rain, the mere rain, was too much to bear. The rain said, *We can wash it all away, all the dirt and all the garbage and all the dust, but not your heartbreak and definitely not what is spoiled inside of you.*

It was worse than anything I'd imagined would befall me if I lost Joanna. It was like she was murdered—disappeared. Certainly she wasn't taking my calls. After a few frantic days I'm lucky anyone still did, and that they not only continued to indulge my sniveling but to offer words of comfort and advice.

Few of those words were productive, of course. There isn't much you can say to a person in hysterical grief that won't sound like a cliché. But there was one suggestion that, surprisingly, did me real good. This was a suggestion from my brother David, whom I called one evening weeping and whining for help. David, who has the patience of a Trappist monk, listened silently for the ten minutes it took me to spend my cache. Then he said, "What you need to do is get dressed, get in your car, and go rent *Singin' in the Rain*."

My first thought was that David was trying to avenge some unspeakable outrage I'd visited upon him in childhood. Rent *Singin' in the Rain*? I'd just lost the woman I loved and he wanted me to watch a movie that centers on the birth of a pure and passionate romance. And with dance numbers! I would die. That's all: I would die. I would lose so much snot and tears in weeping that I'd dehydrate, shrivel up, and die. My roommates would find me days later, hollowed out like a cicada husk on my bed as Gene Kelly and Debbie Reynolds embraced in the Hollywood sun. I couldn't survive such bliss.

But David was insistent. "You'd think that," he said. "You'd think *Singin' in the Rain* would be the absolute last thing you'd want to watch right now. But actually it's the only thing you can watch." *Singin' in the Rain,* David argued, was the only known entertainment in the history of humanity that is totally incapable of causing distress or sadness of any kind. No matter who you are, no matter what emotional condition you are in, no matter your race, religion, ethnicity, socioeconomic status, sexual orientation, or creed, *Singin' in the Rain* will make you forget your worries and smile.

And damn it if he wasn't right. To this day, I've yet to take a pill more miraculous. The entire movie was like some cinematic antidote for neurotic disturbance. To watch it was to be transported for 103 minutes to a universe in which negative emotions have no role except as hurdles tidily jumped on the way to joy—joy of such absurdly high Technicolor wattage that one's own

troubles are washed right out for the duration. Musico-visual Pro-
zac: that's *Singin' in the Rain.*

Now the world knows. Now others can benefit from the insight.
But the American Psychiatric Association shouldn't revise its
treatment guidelines just yet. *Singin' in the Rain* might get you
through an anxious week or two, but it won't get you through
an anxious life. For that you need either a brain transplant (the
only procedure of its kind, it has been said, in which it is better
to be a donor than a recipient), a fully stocked bomb shelter, or a
thorough adjustment of your perspective on existential risk and
reward.

It is possible that the latter would have come to me without
the help of the psychotherapy provided by Brian, whom I began
to see shortly after Joanna and I started having problems. Some
people simply grow less anxious as they grow older. They accumulate their mistakes—the botched love affairs, the blundered
career moves, the bungled ambitions—and they come to learn
that none pulled catastrophe down on their shoulders. They slow
down. They ease up. They develop a more detached, humbled,
amused outlook. For many, anxiety is a young person's vice, a
symptom of idealism, suggests Thoreau, who knew from anxiety
and idealism: "The youth gets together his materials to build
a bridge to the moon, or perchance a palace or temple on the
earth, and at length the middle-aged man concludes to build a
woodshed with them."

But I already knew far too many people over forty to buy much
stock in this hope. And my own anxiety felt far too muscular and
stalwart to expect it to subside without a real struggle. The question, as always, was what I should bring to that struggle, what

methods, what weapons, what skills—and who would teach me
to fight?

Simply perusing the therapist directory supplied by *The Atlan-*
tic had been a daunting experience. What to choose? There
was transpersonal therapy, humanistic therapy, gestalt therapy,
constructivist therapy; Jungian, Adlerian, Kleinian, Rogerian,
Reichian, and Sullivanian therapies; rational emotive behavior
therapy, dialectical behavior therapy, acceptance and commit-
ment therapy, mindfulness-based stress reduction therapy; art
therapy, narrative therapy, dance therapy. It was a crammed field,
and one made all the more confusing by the fact that most therapists aren't theoretically pure; they mix and match from different
orientations according to preference and circumstance.

Every therapist I saw before Brian had taken this magpie approach to my anxiety, and for a long time I had no idea Brian was
different. For a long time, I barely listened to Brian. The anxiety
was too bright and irritating. All I could do was babble, chew on
my cuticles, and plead, quarter-jokingly, to be institutionalized.
Once, just before she ended the relationship, Joanna came to a
session. I dominated, grousing and fulminating for the full fifty
minutes. If you'd taken a time-lapse photograph, Joanna and
Brian would have come out looking like statues, and I like a wisp
of fog.

And yet it wasn't just that I was too desperate to listen to
Brian. It was also that I wasn't desperate enough. "Hitting bottom" is a dubious concept; there always seems to be farther that
one can fall. But after Joanna left I felt an unmistakable acquiescence sweep through me, a sudden apprehension that the old
mechanisms were spent and worthless. I was tired—anxiety is so

tiring!—but I was also disillusioned. I'd tried to make it through on my own and look where it had landed me: no job, no girl, no prospects, and a half-century-old musical eight days late at the video store. It was time to relinquish control.

The previous therapist I'd seen, right out of college, had solidified my understanding of what relinquishing control meant in psychotherapy. Time and again, she faulted me for what she called "defensive intellectualization." She meant I thought too much, and that I used thinking to deflect and avoid therapeutic change. She had a point. I spent a lot of our brief time together sailing in the stratosphere of ideas, unreachable and safe. Where she wanted me was down in the lowlands of family, childhood, memory, trauma.

After Joanna I was finally prepared to muck around in that sump. At last, I thought, I'll lay down my armor and we'll get down to the crux of this anxiety. Brian struck me as shrewder than other therapists. With his interesting beard and his unaffected manner, he reminded me of the Robin Williams character in *Good Will Hunting*—a man who'd call you out on your bullshit, then give you a bear hug. He seemed an ideal partner with whom to attack the really earthy clinical questions: Who screwed me up? Through what actions? Out of what motivations? Who screwed up the people who screwed me up? Was there blame to be assigned? If so, where? Were there resentments still to be digested? If so, which? Was there anger still to be articulated? If so, let's do it now. Let's anatomize my psyche. Let's build a narrative. Let's make a catharsis.

With all this fervor, it was confusing to discover that Brian didn't care about any of this stuff. Every week I took the train from my apartment to the clinic itching to unload a week's worth of memories and feelings, and every week Brian idled away the session staring into his coffee mug or picking lint off his coat. Nothing seemed to reach the man. It was unnerving and disorienting, almost insulting. Finally, when Brian responded with a barely stifled yawn to an expression of the despondency I'd felt upon losing my virginity—a story I was sure would pique his interest—I spoke up.

"I'm sorry. Am I boring you?"

"Oh, excuse me," he said. "No. Go ahead. You were saying."

"What?" I said. "What is it?"

"Nothing. It's nothing. Please, continue."

"What?"

"Well," Brian said. "It's just that . . . you're in pain, right?"

"Yes, I'm in pain. Of course I'm in pain. What are you talking about?"

"You're in active, right-now-as-we-sit-here, present-tense pain."

"Yes," I said. "I'm in active pain. What?"

"It feels like you're in a house, and the house is on fire, and you have to escape right now or you'll burn to death."

"Yes. Exactly. Thank you. That's *exactly* what it feels like."

"OK," he said. "Well, then, if you're in a house that's on fire explain to me the logic of sending in the marshal to figure out what caused the fire. Wouldn't it make more sense to—oh, I don't know—put it out first?"

For a moment, I was dumbfounded. I had the distinct sense that I was being tested. "So you don't want to hear about the lesbians anymore?" I said.

"On the contrary, I'd love to hear about the lesbians," he said. "I'm happy to hear about the lesbians. We can talk about the lesbians, we can talk about your mother, we can talk about your childhood, we can talk about shock therapy or Joanna or books or whatever. We can talk about anything you want to talk about. It's your dollar. I'm just suggesting there might be, maybe, possibly, a better use of your time."

In the past, I had not been pleased with Brian's ideas on how I should use my time. After my article was published, he suggested I spend ten minutes every evening reading the harsh comments on *The Atlantic*'s web site. I lasted twenty seconds the first night and had an anxiety attack that sent me rushing off to hide in the bathtub. Then I unplugged my computer and put it in the closet. Brian tried a few more times to coax me and then concluded, I suspect, that the best tactic was to wait me out. I was an uncommonly stubborn client, but the way I was going it was inevitable I'd submit.

What he suggested to me now was, I realize, not all that different from confronting my detractors. He no longer advised me to go online, but he did advise me to face the direst accusations against myself squarely and thoroughly. It was just that the accusations he now advised me to face were self-generated. *When you feel anxious, what are you thinking?* This was the first question Brian encouraged me to ask myself. *What is going through your head when you feel that icicle form in your chest? What are the thoughts that make you feel so uncomfortable?*

This was not as simple or straightforward an assignment as it may seem. Not only did attending to my own thoughts sound dangerously akin to, say, petting scorpions, the idea that those thoughts preceded the *feeling* of anxiety contradicted everything I knew about how my anxiety and mind operated. The truly gripping thing about anxiety had always been how physical it was. It worked its way into my nerves, my skin, my organs, my hair. Like a fever it infused me. And yet now here came Brian with his mango-colored muttonchops intimating—claiming outright, when I asked him—that it was in fact the exact opposite that was the case. First came the thoughts, then came the feeling. Fever dreams, then fever. A topsy-turvy notion.

"That's not what Freud thought. That's not what Jung thought. That's not what Erikson thought."

"So?" Brian said. "So what?"

"OK then," I said, "if what you say is true then why have I never noticed it happening like that before?"

"Because you haven't been paying close enough attention."

So began a grand experiment in self-exploration. So far as my friends and the IRS were concerned, I spent my days hustling as a freelance journalist: covering aldermen meetings and local-interest stories for the *Globe,* doing a review here and there, fact-checking the odd piece when *The Atlantic* needed an extra hand. But I considered my real work to be keeping a close watch on my cerebral cortex. I didn't want the slightest cognitive fart to escape my notice. As soon as I felt that familiar pulse of anxiety in my body I'd shine a meta-flashlight on myself to test Brian's proposition. Had I been thinking something beforehand? Was it something anxious? Had I spooked myself?

The exercise itself was salutary; it was invigorating to put the self-obsession of anxiety to sanctioned clinical use. The experiment also proved Brian right. The more attention I paid to the mechanics of my anxiety the more I began to notice an aspect of my mind I'd never noticed before—a sort of subconscious chatter, just beneath the surface of awareness, that was always going, always yammering, always commentating, like a little newscaster perched on my frontal lobes. And this newscaster, it turned out, was not the kind of person you'd want to sit next to at a dinner party. He was very pessimistic, my mental homunculus. If there was even a slim chance that a situation could end in calamity, he'd toss it up on the teleprompter and treat it like news. What had happened to the little guy? What was wrong with him?

I had no idea, but at least now I knew the prickly son of a bitch was there, which meant, Brian said, that I could begin to challenge him. All these years my mind had been quietly talking to itself and I hadn't realized it. *Was what it was telling itself true?* This was the second question Brian encouraged me to ask myself. *Listen closely. When you are anxious note precisely what your mind has said and then interrogate what you find for accuracy. Treat every anxious thought like a philosophical proposition and test it. Apply logic to the content of your mind.*

I first took this advice, or found the courage to take it, on a Tuesday afternoon while waiting for an editor to call me back. I pulled up *The Atlantic*'s homepage and, before I could reconsider the wisdom of what I was about to do, I navigated to the public forum for my article. As before, it took just one negative comment—in this case, the designation of the article as "libelous"—to unleash a cascade of anxiety into my system. The impulse to recoil was tremendous. But I forced myself to stay at my desk and tease out what I had thought in the millisecond just after reading the comment and just before becoming frantic. It didn't take long to determine that what I'd thought was this: *The commenter is right. The article is libelous.* Once I'd made this discovery I took a deep breath and asked myself the next prescribed question: Was the article really libelous? After all, the word "libel" isn't like the word "stupid" or "rude"; it has a formal, static definition. I got out my *Webster's* and looked it up.

libel (lī′bel) *n.* [[ME, little book < OFr < L *libellus*, little book, writing, lampoon, dim. of *liber*, a book: see LIBRARY]] **1** any false

and malicious written or printed statement, or any sign, picture,
or effigy, tending to expose a person to public ridicule, hatred, or
contempt or to injure a person's reputation in any way

On this basis, it was indisputable that the article as a whole
was not libelous; it had been fact-checked according to the
magazine's rigorous standards. Possibly an error had slipped in
or eluded inspection, possibly that error had exposed a person
to ridicule or contempt or injured his or her reputation. But had
there been any malice in the theoretical error? No. Impossible. I
had written the article in good faith, no matter what else could
be said about me. Ergo, there could be no libel. My anxiety had
stemmed from a false premise.

It was like defusing a mental bomb, and Brian intended for
me to apply the method boldly, to shy from no potential reality.
Take the usual existential-ruin line of thought, the one that begins with an innocuous choice—white or whole wheat, scrambled
or poached, orange or grapefruit—and spins off into a fantasy of
poverty, homelessness, disease, shame, death. Brian didn't want
me to dismiss these possibilities. It's a funny life; anything could
happen. But if I was going to insist on entertaining disaster sce-
narios, I at least had to be honest about the probabilities. Yes, a
particular breakfast order could *conceivably* lead, by a series of
logical steps, to the total derailment of my hopes and prospects.
Yet even I had to admit that the chances were slim. It didn't take
a sociologist to confirm that well-educated, upper-middle-class
Jews seldom end up sleeping in dumpsters. And if I was an exception to the rule? If I did end up alone, disease-ravaged, and dead?

"Well," Brian would say cheerfully, "at least then you won't be
anxious anymore!"

15.

digging a trench

I wasn't with Brian long as these things go, just over a year. As the summer approached I concluded it was time to leave Boston for New York. Joanna and I lived less than two miles from each other. I was starting to hear rumors of her dating. I imagined large, resolute men with steroidal forearms and short haircuts—Navy SEAL types. That and the crematorium around the corner from my apartment kept me in a somber mood even when my anxiety was dormant.

New York seemed the more natural place for me anyway. I told anyone who asked that I quit *The Atlantic* because fact-checking didn't leave me time to pursue my writing. It was a lie that forced a life. Being home all day was repellent: all that quiet downtime, all that envy of the gainfully employed and fully insured. I didn't dare get a job, however, for fear that it would make me look foolish, and that it might be worse. Through a combination of timidity, pride, and inertia I thus became a professional writer, and professional writers, I believed, should live in New York. It helped that David, Scott, and my mother were all still there. It might be nice—I was shocked to hear myself think this—to be around family again.

I didn't tell Joanna I was leaving Boston. Having persuaded her to make the opposite move, I doubted she would take the news kindly—if she would even agree to see me. And I still doubted my ability to treat her with solicitude and kindness. Applying Brian's suggestions was proving to be arduous, creeping work, and I was devoted to it above all other considerations. If anxiety woke me at 3 a.m., I got out of bed, turned on the lights, and x-rayed my dreams to see what they'd said. If anxiety struck me in the grocery store, I abandoned my cart in the aisle and used the long walk home to set myself right. If anxiety struck during an interview, I excused myself, went to the bathroom, and sat on the toilet seat until I'd identified and analyzed my thoughts. Why shouldn't I make myself my priority? It was the one perk to being alone. With no one to be responsible for or to, no one to have to please or gratify or even talk to, I could indulge my needs as much as I wanted. I could convert my life into an emergency room, and myself into both doctor and patient.

A new solipsism to replace the old solipsism: the irony didn't escape me. But I didn't much care about irony anymore. I was weary of complexity and doubleness, fed up with the knotted and the thorny. Around that time I came across what Freud had to say about anxiety. He called it "the nodal point at which the most various and important questions converge, a riddle whose solution would be bound to throw a flood of light upon our whole mental existence." *Well, Herr Doctor, I* thought, *you can have the various and important questions. I just want a little peace. If that means being entombed in myself for a while longer, so be it.*

I left in late June. When I called my editor at the *Globe* to say good-bye, he said, "You're a promising young writer, but I'm not sure we got the very best of you."

"Ha ha," I replied.

Because Brian was so prescriptive a therapist, I was able to carry him with me to New York. I was never in doubt as to what I was supposed to do. Nor was I ever in doubt that what I was supposed to do was correct—that it fit the facts and that it would work. I could feel it working. With each instance of neutralized anxiety the little newscaster in my head got just a little less negative, a little less insistent. His wild subliminal rants played at fewer times, and had less demagogic power over me when they did.

One night, a few months after I'd moved, I cut my finger trying to slice an English muffin. The cut was severe. I could see the pink of deep tissue and beneath it the bone. A year earlier I would have had instant visions of disaster—the night, the week, and in turn an entire existence ruined by a hasty gesture. I would have abused myself mercilessly for my stupidity. Now I just stood in the kitchen watching the blood drip into the sink, thinking, *Well, that just happened. Better do something about it.* And then I allowed myself a moment of quiet pride, for such matter-of-fact poise and practicality—such *reflexive* poise and practicality— signaled a momentous shift in my mental life. When they wove the stitches in, I almost smiled.

I have never been less anxious than I was during that first year in New York, even as the lawsuit against me was filed and

I struggled to find work, pay my bills, and get over Joanna. For the first time in memory, daily life felt unencumbered and fluid. Natural. I thought I was cured.

I didn't yet realize that there is no cure for anxiety, just perpetual treatment. I didn't yet realize that a quarter century of anxiety had gouged deep, packed-earth ruts in my brain, and that the only way to stop my thoughts from falling back into those ruts was to dig new tracks and keep digging them, forever. I didn't yet realize that the only nonnegotiable approach to the anxious life is discipline.

So it has been that, over and over again, through the years, I have relapsed and returned, relapsed and returned. With no perfect discipline the relapses are inevitable, but I have learned to take measures so that they don't last as long as they once did, and so that the returns last longer and are less volatile. I have learned that the best safeguards against nervous collapse are responsibilities: jobs, contracts, assignments, and, above all, the blessed, bracing restraints of human relationships.

Joanna helped to teach me that. She moved back to New York a year after I did, landing, by dumb chance, in an apartment only five blocks from my own. At first this upset me deeply. Joanna was a living reminder of the terrible losses my anxiety could effect, the hells of indecisiveness it could conjure. It was painful enough that, through my sister-in-law and mutual friends, I was privy to occasional dispatches about her comings and goings. Now I had to worry about bumping into her at the corner bodega. Just a glimpse of her, I feared, would set me back months.

I avoided her. We avoided each other. Who wants to relive the failed past? Then another year passes, another year of ebbing and cresting anxiety, and my subconscious pulled a fast one. I dreamed of her.

We were at a circus or carnival in the country, holding hands at the center of a flat and crowded fairgrounds. All around us, kicking up dirt, were jugglers, stilt-walkers, fire-eaters, funambulists. There were tremendous elephants teetering on red-and-white balls. There were sleek white horses in tinkling silver finery. There were acrobatic monkeys in gaudy jesters' clothes, diving and looping and baring their canines. I couldn't see Joanna, but I could smell the soap on her skin and feel her thumb gently rubbing mine, a smooth rhythm in the chaos.

I woke up confused and clammy. In the trashcan by the bed were the remnants of the three-dollar pork enchilada I'd had for dinner the night before. I kicked off the covers, vowed never again to buy Mexican food from an establishment owned by Koreans, and went out for a run to get Joanna out of my head.

But she wouldn't leave. All through the morning I sat at my desk fidgeting and neglecting my work, trying to shake the clingy dream-feel of Joanna and me side by side in the middle of all that mayhem. I spent the afternoon the same way. In the evening I took another run. Then I went to the movies. Then I got drunk. Then I threw up. Nothing helped. First thing the next morning, I called Kate.

"I'm in huge trouble," I told her. "I think I'm in love with my ex-girlfriend."

Kate forbade me from making a move. "Do *not* call Joanna," she said. "It wouldn't be fair. This might just be your anxiety or your guilt playing tricks on you. Or loneliness. Promise me you'll wait a week. If she's still on your mind we'll get together and talk it out."

A week later Kate and I met for dinner at a restaurant downtown, an austere bistro with obscenely high ceilings and polished concrete floors. I was unshaven and there was a large soup stain on my shirt.

"It's not that bad," Kate said.

"It's hopeless. Not even worth trying. I told her I didn't love her anymore in Venice. Venice! Women don't like hearing that, but they especially don't like hearing it in Venice."

"Maybe she still has feelings for you, too."

"Don't patronize me, please. Did I ever tell you how a month after she dumped me I showed up at her door blubbering for forgiveness? She acted like I had scabies."

"So what are you going to do?"

"I don't have a choice. I'm going to move to South America. I have to start learning Spanish."

After we ordered, Kate spotted a friend sitting at the bar, a handsome, long-faced man reading a book and nursing a glass of red wine. He was an architect and author she had once done research for, and she said he'd been in a similar romantic predicament. He had dated a young woman for a year or so and then, out of a desire to play the field, broken it off. Some months later he realized that he loved her. He'd made a terrible mistake. By that time, however, she was with someone else, someone younger, and was unmoved by his remorse.

"That's awful," I said. "What happened?"

"Oh, they have a great apartment about three blocks from here. She's six months pregnant with their first child."

I demanded an introduction and squeezed in at the bar. I told the man everything, from Joanna and I meeting at my brother's party to my horrendous anxieties to our trip to Italy to my ongoing treatment and self-treatment to my recent dream and renewed obsession. He nodded as if he understood it all perfectly. When I was finally done, I asked him what I should do. What advice could he give me?

He thought for a moment, then looked at me intently and said: "Dig a trench."

"What?" I said. "Dig a what?"

"You have to dig a trench and wait. As long as it takes. She has no reason to trust you. You've been neurotic, crazy. Call it anxious, fine, but to her you just come off as an asshole. Why should she choose you? Why would she even listen? Your words don't mean a thing anymore. You have to show her that you can behave well. You have to show her that you're a stable, loving person. And that means digging in and doing it, really doing it, for as long as it takes to win her back. Being her friend first and foremost. But you better mean it. You better be able to really deliver, 'cause it sounds like you've caused this girl some pretty bad heartache already."

"But what if it doesn't work? What if I don't win her back?"

"You might not. What do you want, a guarantee? There isn't any. This is the best deal you're going to get. But be prepared. Even if it does work it'll probably take a while."

"How long did it take you?"

"A year," he said. "The most important year of my life."

Joanna was merciful. She took me back after four months. I never pushed the matter; I never coaxed. I just showed up and was kind and quietly attentive. Like the architect's girlfriend, Joanna had moved on to someone else. I willed myself not to be jealous. I practiced being patient and still.

In due course the other guy faded and the moment came. When we kissed for the first time—again—Joanna pulled away and said, "Are you still nuts?"

"Yes," I said. "I'm afraid so. But I'm working on it."

"How do I know you won't freak out again? How do I know I'm not being stupid?"

I told her I undoubtedly would freak out again, numerous times. It was unavoidable. Freaking out is who I am. But I promised her, hand solemnly in the air, that my anxiety would never again infect her or us as it had in the past. I would make certain of it.

Two years later, Joanna and I were married. I have struggled to keep my promise to her, but for the most part I have kept it. When I slip back into anxious rumination, I keep it to myself, or off-load it on Kate and others who don't have to live with me. I take the time to reacquaint myself with Brian's methods, which I now know to have a name—cognitive therapy—and a worldwide popularity. I meditate. I read *The Book of Scott* and the scattered bits of wisdom and comfort I've gathered on my own over the years. I even do my mother's breathing exercises.

And when nothing else works, I recall a little perspective-shifting trick Brian taught me just before I came around to doing the real therapeutic work. It was a simple trick—silly, really. I almost refused to do it. But something told me I should try, and I'm grateful I did.

Here was the trick: Whenever I felt my mind tracing dire consequences again, Brian said, whenever I felt it spinning out its cruel, imaginative horrors, simply lift my eyes, raise my hands, and shout, "Bring it on! Lemme see what you've got!"

It would be impossible to exaggerate how foolish I felt when I agreed to try this. I was standing in the middle of Brian's office, trembling as usual. My underarms were stained with sweat. The palms of my hands and the bottoms of my feet were damp, as was my forehead and the small of my back and the backs of my knees. The only dry thing about me was my mouth, which felt as if it were carved out of balsa wood. I went through with it anyway.

I lifted my arms above my head, I set my sights on the clinic's dotted, dropped-tile ceiling, and I challenged God, the universe, the Fates, or the Furies—whatever or whomever I was meant to be addressing—to come at me with everything there is. *Bring it on.*

Odd, the surge of terror that struck me upon beginning. For all my solid disbelief, at that moment I was as certain that there is something omniscient and vengeful out there as an eighteenth-century Hasidic Jew, a ritual slaughterer, I once read about. This Hasid used to weep bitterly every time he left his wife and children to go to work, as if he were setting off each morning to attend his own execution. When he was asked why this was, he explained that when he began his work he cried out to God. Who could say that God wouldn't strike him dead before he had a chance to cry out, "Have mercy on us!"

What was odder than my terror upon beginning, however, was what happened when I was done.

I laughed.

Despite myself, I laughed.

It wasn't much of a laugh. It lasted maybe a second before I was again enveloped in my anxiety. I can't even say if it was audible or not. What it was, certainly, was unexpected—as unexpected as if the roof of the clinic had suddenly cracked open to reveal a beam of sunlight aimed in my direction. Laughter? I hadn't laughed in months. Totally dried up. I figured I was done with laughter. What did I have to laugh about? Why was everyone always finding existence so damned funny? How could you possibly laugh when any minute your mind might sprout horns and fangs and a vicious temper? Laughter was for the ignorant. It wasn't for the anxious.

Yet there I was, laughing. What had come over me? I had no idea.

I think I have an idea now. I think I understand now why I laughed, and as often as possible I try to remember why. I laughed, I think, because in return for my grudging stunt of cosmic defiance I received . . . nothing. Nothing. I rang the bell and no one answered the door. My little spasm of pre-invocation terror had been in vain, and so, by extension, had been all my terror. What was there to be anxious about? Many things. *Many* things. Death, sickness, loss, failure, success, poverty, violence, insanity, dismemberment, disfigurement. How many of those scourges afflicted me now? None. How many were designed to afflict me personally? None. I was alone, the dogged architect of my own humdrum degradations.

What a fool.

ABOUT THE AUTHOR

Daniel Smith is the author of *Muses, Madmen, and Prophets: Hearing Voices and the Borders of Sanity*. His essays and articles have appeared in numerous publications, including *The Atlantic, Granta, n+1, New York, The New York Times Magazine,* and *Slate*. Smith has taught at Bryn Mawr and The College of New Rochelle, where he holds the Mary Ellen Donnelly Critchlow Endowed Chair in English.

SIMON & SCHUSTER PAPERBACKS
READING GROUP GUIDE

monkey mind

daniel smith

ABOUT THIS GUIDE

This reading group guide for *Monkey Mind* includes an introduction, discussion questions, ideas for enhancing your book club, and a Q&A with author Daniel Smith. The suggested questions are intended to help your reading group find new and interesting angles and topics for your discussion. We hope that these ideas will enrich your conversation and increase your enjoyment of the book.

INTRODUCTION

Monkey Mind is a memoir of one man's life of anxiety and his quest to both understand and overcome it.

Anxiety once paralyzed Daniel Smith, causing him to chew his cuticles until they bled. It has dogged his days, threatened his sanity, and ruined his relationships.

In *Monkey Mind,* Smith articulates what it is like to live with anxiety, demystifying the disease with humor and evocatively expressing its self-destructive absurdities. With honesty and wit, Smith shares his own hilarious and heart-wrenching story of anxiety and how he was finally able to tame the affliction.

TOPICS & QUESTIONS FOR DISCUSSION

1. Smith begins *Monkey Mind* with two epigraphs, one from *The Woman in White* that reads, in part, "We all say it's on the nerves, and we none of us know what we mean when we say it," and one from Nabokov's "Signs and Symbols" that reads, "Everything is a cipher and of everything he is the theme." Discuss both of these epigraphs within the context of Smith's memoir. How do they set up his discussion of anxiety and inform your reading of *Monkey Mind*?

2. Discuss the book's title. Why do you think that Smith chose it? What does it mean to have a "monkey mind"?

3. In the introduction to *Monkey Mind*, Smith says, "I was anxiety personified." (p. 7) What do you think he means? Given what you know about Daniel at this stage of his memoir, do you agree with his self-assessment? Why or why not?

4. When Smith visits a therapist while he is in college and is asked for the reason behind his visit, he says, "I suffer from anxiety." This is the first time that he has "said it like that before. I'd never used the word in that kind of sentence." (p. 129) Why do you think that Smith chooses to describe his motivation for seeking help in the way that he does? Do you think that the change in phrasing also suggests a change in the way that he views his problem? How so?

5. Smith says anxiety "is after all a relationship of a sort." (p. 74) What do you think he means by this statement? In what ways

do you see Daniel's life dominated by anxiety? Were any of those ways surprising to you?

6. Esther plays a huge role in Daniel's life. What are your impressions of her based on Daniel's descriptions? Why do you think that Daniel develops a friendship with her despite his reservations? What are the results of the friendship?

7. According to Smith, "In love, anxiety takes victims." (p. 182) How does this statement play out in regard to his relationship with Joanna? Do you see it playing out in other relationships of Daniel's? Which ones and how?

8. Of his childhood, Smith says, "Even then it was possible that I wouldn't become my mother." (p. 37) Describe Marilyn. In what ways would Daniel shy away from being like her? What do you think of her ability to manage her anxiety?

9. Were you surprised that Daniel confides in his mother about his first sexual experience? Why or why not? How do each of his parents react to what he has told them?

10. According to Smith, "The truly gripping thing about anxiety had always been how physical it was." (p. 199) Describe some of the corporeal ways in which Smith's anxiety manifests itself. Were any particularly surprising to you? If any, which ones?

11. Daniel Smith includes a self-portrait that William James drew in his youth during a bout with anxiety and depression. (p. 119) Why do you think that Smith chose to include this image in his memoir? What does it show you about Smith's own mental state?

12. In listing jobs that an anxiety sufferer should avoid at all costs, Smith includes "fact-checker at a major American magazine." (p. 147) Discuss Smith's own experiences working as a fact-checker. Why does it seem to be a bad idea? Knowing what you do about anxiety after reading *Monkey Mind*, are there other jobs that you would add to Smith's jobs-to-be-avoided list?

13. Although Daniel Smith sees a therapist while he is living in Boston, he says, "it wasn't just that I was too desperate to listen to Brian. It was also that I wasn't desperate enough." (p. 196) What is it that eventually makes Smith more receptive to Brian's help? How do Brian's methods differ from those of the other therapists that Daniel has seen? What's the result?

ENHANCE YOUR BOOK CLUB

1. Daniel Smith says, "When I found Roth, I felt I had found my anxiety's Rosetta Stone." (p. 136) Read one of Philip Roth's books with your book club and discuss the role that anxiety plays. Discuss why Smith might have found Roth's books to be a balm.

2. Smith's in-depth article about electroshock therapy, titled "Shock and Disbelief," which appeared in *The Atlantic* in 2001, was both a professional triumph and a personal disaster. Read the original article here: http://www.theatlantic.com/magazine/archive/2001/02/shock-and-disbelief/302114/. Then, discuss the complaint against Smith.

3. To learn more about Daniel Smith, read about his other work, read reviews of *Monkey Mind*, and find anxiety resources, visit his official site at http://monkeymindchronicles.com.

A CONVERSATION WITH DANIEL SMITH

1. **It seems as if *Monkey Mind* existed in your mind for some time. What prompted you to write it? And why at this particular juncture in your career?**
   I was looking for something to do that had more narrative and that was more comical than my previous work, which was often journalistic and based in a lot of research. My experience with anxiety not only fit those needs perfectly, but I noticed that no one had really written a book like the one I wanted to write—one that explained, with as much sensitivity and accuracy (and necessary humor) as possible what anxiety actually *feels* like. I wanted to answer the question, What's it like to go through life with a body and mind hard-wired for systemic doubt?

2. **In countless consumer reviews on Goodreads, readers mention that *Monkey Mind* helped them understand their own anxiety or that of loved ones, and *Psychology Today* said, "If you're chronically anxious and want to better explain to a loved one what you're going through, hand them *Monkey Mind*." Did you set out to write a book that would help others deal with their own anxiety?**
   I set out to write a book that would describe anxiety well and as an *experience,* not necessarily as a pathology. I think this aspect of the book is what people have responded to most and found most helpful. I'm delighted by this.

3. **Writing *Monkey Mind* required you to revisit some of your low points in dealing with your anxiety. Was the experience therapeutic? Or did reliving some of your anxiety attacks stir up those feelings again?**

There were moments when writing about my past difficulties with anxiety stirred up old worries, but these moments were surprisingly rare for the same reason, I think, that I didn't really find any therapeutic value in the experience—because the day-to-day problems involved in writing *Monkey Mind* were literary and not clinical: how to tell the story well, how to describe something so elusive and complex, what to put in and what to leave out, where to put this comma or that semi-colon, etc. I like to keep things separate: writing at the writing desk, therapy at the therapist's office.

4. Aaron T. Beck praised *Monkey Mind*, saying it "does for anxiety what William Styron's *Darkness Visible* did for depression." Did *Darkness Visible* inspire you in your writing? What other books and writers influenced you?
I greatly admire *Darkness Visible*—it's a powerful and vivid book—but I didn't have it in mind as a model when I was writing *Monkey Mind*. Indeed, I didn't have any models in mind. I did, however, find myself repeatedly drawn to certain works of literature. Nabokov's marvelous short story "Signs and Symbols," for example. For some reason I can't explain (and don't even really want to), I couldn't stop reading that story. I turned to it almost daily. I also found myself turning to the biographies of great writers and thinkers who have experienced anxiety, foremost among them William James, Alice James, Kierkegaard, and Kafka.

5. Your mother was very supportive of your decision to write *Monkey Mind*, even when it meant that you were exposing her own dealings with anxiety. Were you surprised by her reaction?
I was and I wasn't. On the one hand, although my mother is a psychotherapist who specializes in treating anxiety, she

can be very private about her own struggles with anxiety and panic. (Perhaps her reticence is *because* she's a therapist: she has to be tactful about what she does and doesn't divulge to her patients.) On the other hand, she is a bold, brave, and unapologetic person with an almost perverse hatred of secrecy. I think she knew that the book could be useful and comforting to people, and she wanted to be part of that.

6. **Many reviews have praised *Monkey Mind* for its humor. *O Magazine* said "You'll laugh out loud many times" and, in a four star review, *People* calls it "unforgettable, surprisingly hilarious." Although you are recounting your own struggles with illness, your depictions are often very funny. Was that always your intention? What did you hope to achieve by inserting comedy into your memoir?**

I always knew that a book about anxiety (at least any book about anxiety that I wrote) would have to be funny. The reason for this is quite simply that anxiety *is* funny. It's painful, too, of course—very painful, as well as destructive to lives in all sorts of ways. But the way anxiety causes pain and destruction is through absurdity. It inflates niggling fears and reconfigures the nervous system in a way that, even while you're going through it, you know is overwrought. You know you're being tricked somehow. So to write about anxiety in a comic mode (though not just in a comic mode) is a way of both acknowledging the absurdity of anxiety and of disempowering the experience just a bit. It's a way of reasserting control for that moment of humor.

7. **Your experience in the aftermath of the publication of "Shock and Disbelief" in *The Atlantic* was particularly harrowing, kicking off a huge anxiety attack. After that**

experience, have you shied away from reading reviews of your writing? How do you handle the possibility of criticism?

I haven't shied away from reading criticism of my work, but I have learned, largely because of that episode, not to become paralyzed by criticism. There happens to be a lot you can learn from how people react to your writing; I learned a lot from how people reacted to that particular article. But you have to be selective about what criticism you deem actionable, and you always have to remember that you can't go back. What's published is published. All that matters is the work that's in front of you.

8. **Your initial year at Brandeis was particularly fraught and filled with severe anxiety attacks. It was also there that you first articulated that you suffered from anxiety. Following the publication of *Monkey Mind*, you returned to Brandeis University, this time speaking at an event co-sponsored by the Psychological Counseling Center, the creative writing department of Brandeis, and *Brandeis Magazine*. What was it like to return to the place you once called "the epicenter of anxiety"?**

It was, remarkably, a somewhat cathartic trip. I never felt particularly comfortable or settled at Brandeis. But returning after nearly fifteen years was, to my surprise and delight, very much like coming home. There was no spasm of nerves, no reignition of old anxieties. There was just a sense of gratitude and pleasure at being back in this place I knew so well and where I learned so much. But the administration did put out baked goods at the event, so maybe that helped.

9. **What has been the most rewarding aspect of publishing *Monkey Mind*?**

It has been a great pleasure to hear from so many people who say to me, "I've given your book to my husband/wife/father/mother/boyfriend/girlfriend/brother/sister as a way to explain what I feel but can't describe."

10. **Early in *Monkey Mind*, you say "This is no recovery memoir, let me warn you" (p. 14), and yet, by the end of the book, you've managed to find a strategy to help you keep your anxiety in check. Do you consider yourself to be in recovery? What advice would you give readers who are struggling with anxiety?**

I don't consider myself to be in recovery because I don't think anxiety is something a person can—or should—"recover" from. Anxiety isn't just a problem; it's an emotion, and a universal and adaptive one at that. We need anxiety in order to survive, both as individuals and as a species. That said, I am far less overwhelmed by anxiety than I once was and far more capable of keeping my anxiety in check. My experience tells me that this is because I came to think of anxiety as something very like a habit: a way of thinking and feeling that I could, with effort and dedication, learn to change.

11. **What's next for you as a writer? Since your memoir was so well received, are you considering writing more?**

I'm working on a number of different projects, including some fiction and some criticism. And, to my surprise, I might not be totally done with anxiety. I find myself increasingly interested in the cultural aspects of the experience. What is it that makes not just a person but a culture anxious? How does anxiety spread? Why do so many people seem to suffer from anxiety at this particular point in time? I've been asking myself these questions and seeing where they lead me.